CALL OF THE QUAIL

CALL OF THE QUAIL

A Tribute to the Gentleman Game Bird

COUNTRYSPORT PRESS
Selma, Alabama

© 1989 by Countrysport, Inc.

Published by Countrysport, Inc., Craig Industrial Park, Bldg 116, Selma, AL 36701

Printed in the United States of America
Second Printing 1999

Library of Congress Catalog Card Number: 89-060725

ISBN 0-924357-03-7

Dedication

To George Herbert Walker Bush,
Forty-first President of the United States

Contents

Introduction

This book is something of a landmark in sporting literature – an original anthology.

So often these days, previously published pieces revolving around a central theme are gathered up and offered in a new form – old material, new binding. That's not to say that doing things that way is necessarily bad, it's just that a lot of folks feel that some of the best writers who have ever parked themselves behind a typewriter are alive, well, and writing today. We agree.

Call of the Quail is, indeed, a tribute to the gentleman game bird: the bobwhite quail. He is, for countless thousands of us, what dogs and guns and frosty mornings are all about. We may be Midwestern farmers or Southern plantation owners; we may live in big cities or small towns, and we may even be Yankee quail hunters who take a shooting vacation to the South every year. We follow, variously, pointers, setters,

Brittanies, shorthairs, wirehairs, and farm collies with a knack for finding quail. Our guns go from taped-up pumps to London Bests. Doesn't matter – we are brothers under the skin.

And of these brothers, none are finer than the writers assembled here. Each is called by the bobwhite in his own, unique way. I'd like to tell you a little about them.

Charles Dickey has been chasing quail and thinking about quail and writing about quail since he can remember. His home in the South gives him ample opportunity to slake his thirst for covey rises and brown broom sedge. Charley is one of the fraternity's truly funny people, although in "Meet the Gentleman Game Bird" he handles a serious topic, but with typical Dickey flair. His books and magazine articles have delighted and enriched an entire generation of shooters.

Rocky Evans adds his notes on the future of bobwhites. Rocky is Executive Director of Quail Unlimited, one of the country's fastest-growing wildlife organizations, one he founded in the early 1980s. Rocky is the man to give an accurate appraisal of the future of this fine game bird as the century winds into its final decade.

Tom Huggler is the author of another quail book, and one of the few people to have gunned every species of quail in the United States. His knowledge of the bird comes from having spent years hunting them, and one solid year doing nothing but traveling, researching, photographing, and meeting the people who hunt quail. His favorite area is the great Midwest, so it was only natural that he write the chapter entitled "Quail in the Heartland." Tom's skills as a writer are quickly evident and well-known, especially to those who have followed him through his hundreds of magazine articles and many books. His writing on quail is also a social commentary on the Midwest, its people, its land. For Tom, the hunt is often only half the reason he is there.

Michael McIntosh, as serious students of shotgunning know, is among the half-dozen or so real experts on shooting and shotguns in this country. Mac lives in Missouri and despite trips north for woodcock and grouse, and forays west for sharptails and pheasants, bobwhites remain his favorite. A former university professor, Mac also spent a good share of his career in the wildlife business. But shotguns and shooting are his first love, and any frosty morning in season is likely to find Mac, his Brittany "October," and his vintage A.H. Fox shotgun ambling along a fencerow or bashing through a plumthicket in good quail country.

Quail hunting is nothing without the dogs, and *Dr. Jim Nelson* adds a wealth of knowledge on that subject. He is the country doctor in Elm Creek, Nebraska and a highly skilled physician and surgeon who could probably have a huge practice in a big city, but that would take him away from his quail hunting and dog training. Doc owns and operates Plumthicket Kennels, and the last time I was there, he was training some breeds of dogs most of us have never heard of. He regularly haunts the South as well as the Midwest for quail.

David Simpson, from Texas, is an admitted bobwhite quail chaser of immeasurable devotion. During the long Texas season, he will hunt two or three times a week; he prefers the bobwhite to all other birds. His writing is some of the best currently being produced – scholarly and intellectual, but with a flair and warmth that mark him as one of the top of the "new breed."

One of America's favorite sporting writers, and one of my favorite people, is *Charles Waterman*, author of the chapter on plantation quail hunting. Charlie is a book author, magazine columnist, dog man, and world traveler. But most of all, he is a quail hunter. Like Huggler, Charlie has taken the quail "Grand Slam," but bobwhites in the traditional style remain a passion. Charlie's observations on the sporting scene in this country are well-known, and his home in the South allows him the chance to scratch his quail itch whenever it occurs.

Finally, this book wouldn't be what it is without the illustrative work of Texas artist *Herb Booth*. A premier sporting artist, Herb is also a quail buff, fine shot, and keen dog man. His understanding of the subject comes through in the watercolor and pencil work he executes here so expertly.

Thanks to these men, and thanks to you who care for this fine little bird. May his tribe increase.

•   •   •

I am a nearly psychotic collector of "stuff." I've got duck-hunting stuff and grouse-hunting stuff, and stuff for rainy days and cold days and hot days, and stuff for the odd exotic excursion all ready to go.

For example, I've got the right gun, boots, shooting coat, and tweed hat all set in case I ever get the chance to shoot walked-up snipe on an Irish bog. So far, nobody's stopped by with the offer, but if they do, I know just where I can lay my hands on just the right stuff.

As a Yankee born and more or less raised, it seems a little funny that I might have a good portion of my outdoor impedimenta devoted to bobwhite quail, but I do. That's because at the end of any given season over the last decade, I've spent more time, shotshells, and money on quail than any other game bird. I've even got a for-sure quail gun. And not just *any* quail gun, mind you. I've got a – now pay attention – early season, close cover, over-steady-dogs sixteen gauge that's as fast as lightning. The chances of my hitting anything with it are about the same as Libya being named the 51st state, but that doesn't count. When I show up with it, I look like a real sport, which is what really matters.

I don't know how it happened, exactly, but I ended up hunting quail last year in Iowa, Nebraska, Tennessee, Texas, and Georgia (twice). But since quail aren't really all that common up here where I live, I just don't consider myself an *authentic* quail hunter like the men in this book.

I don't have a real quail dog, for example. I've got an English setter who will hunt quail when I take her along, but that's not often. Mainly I enjoy hunting with the other fellow's dog and letting him squirm when the dog eats the first four birds we shoot or rolls in something dead.

My dog does better on ruffed grouse and woodcock, so she goes a little brain-dead when she encounters a running covey. I took her to Iowa once for quail, and the open spaces gave her the jitters. She's used to being hemmed in by thick stuff in the coverts, and the only time she was happy and productive was down in a brushy draw.

And, there's the snakes. A Yankee dog like mine doesn't know anything about snakes except for the odd garter snake she polishes off in the backyard in the summer. She sure doesn't know about snakes with long fangs and short fuses, and she's getting a little too old for me to start teaching her. Instead, I'd rather hunt with snake-broke dogs who know the score.

Speaking of snakes, it seems as though half my quail stuff is really snake stuff. Taking up most of the room are a pair of snake boots and a pair of snake leggings that make me feel like I'm hunting in a couple of stovepipes. The truth is, I rarely wear the snake boots even in snake country, though I should. But I've been pretty lucky in not seeing many rattlers or cottonmouths. I know – it's the ones you don't see that cause the problem, but for now I depend on chilly weather and dumb luck to keep my hide unpunctured. Still, I *do* spend a lot of time looking at the ground.

Some of the other stuff includes shooting vests and hats, many decked out in the almost-mandatory blaze orange so that my hunting partners won't have a hard time distinguishing my stationary backside from a six-ounce bird in flight. Blaze orange bothers me – not the *idea* of it, but the color. Seems as though white would do just as well, as it did for years, but most places and states want you decked out like you're directing traffic through Interstate 80 construction, so we do what we have to do. I guess all of this is a way of saying that bobwhite quail have a strong hold on us, a hold that makes us risk unfamiliar places and conditions for a few days of grand shooting.

Some of the best stuff I have are photographs of some of the places I've been lucky enough to get to and some of the friends I've shared those times with. I've got one picture of Mike McIntosh posing with his gun in hand and his foot on my chest as I'm stretched out flat on my back on a grassy hill in Iowa. We'd been hunting all day on some Conservation Reserve Program Land (we decided that the initials for the program should be reordered into "CPR" land), and Mac took advantage of the opportunity to go for the cheap laugh.

Another set of photos features one of the real characters I've ever met: Ray Gene Hall of Pinefield's Plantation. Ray Gene is the head guide there, down in the plantation country around south Georgia, and he made the trip worth it even if the shooting hadn't been as great as it was.

Ray Gene keeps up a constant conversation with everyone at the same time, and he listens attentively when you've got a funny story to tell or a question about why the dog is doing this or that.

One afternoon, Ray Gene and another guide had been talking about which of our party of four was the best shot, and they boiled it down to two young chargers and placed a little wager on "their men." They set it up so that these two could shoot the same covey rises for an afternoon that we all spent hunting from the mule-drawn wagon. The other guide, J.B., was sure his man would take a double on the rise, and Ray Gene was equally convinced his man would emerge the better shot. The two shooters, of course, didn't know there was a contest going on at all – they were just enjoying a mid-winter quail hunt in the old, grand manner.

Well, J.B.'s man outshot Ray Gene's on the first covey and the next, and the next. When he did it a fourth time, Ray Gene wordlessly handed over the cash, hopped down from the wagon where he'd been perched watching the shooters, and started toward a handy persimmon tree. J.B. asked, "Where ya goin'?"

Says Ray Gene: "Gonna cut me a switch."

There's the picture I have of Dave Meisner on a quail hunt in Texas riding to the field we were to hunt on the front hood of a Jeep. Dave's talking with me and posing nicely for the camera, not knowing that about two feet to his left is a big, ornery, curious range bull, trotting alongside to get a better look.

But then, I guess we've all got our own pictures, even if they're just in our minds.

What about the pictures we carry with us of coveys coming up with the clattering buzz and roar that defies the words we use to describe it? Every time is just like the first, and the wing-wash steals our breath away.

Or what about the picture you have of that first double, both birds cartwheeling down from twin globes of feathers? And did you follow that covey up or let it go in celebration?

What of that hunt you took in Kansas and that prairie blizzard that caught you by surprise three miles from the truck? Was it anything like the time you drove all night to Iowa and found the roads washed out?

Have you watched the touch of gray start to come to your shooting buddy? Have the two of you hunted together through a half-dozen good dogs, kids graduating from high school, and grandchildren? Do you try to remember what he looked like when you walked in on your first covey together, and will he always be that way to you – young and full of fire for the hunt? And what a surprise to find out that what the ninety-year-old said once is true: "Inside – here – I'm still eighteen."

Do you carry mental pictures of a pup's first covey find – straight, tall, trembling – or an old-timer's last single, nailed with the skill of years that have taken their toll, the puppy within him trembling still? We know, the dogs and us, when that last hunt has come. The dogs pretend they don't, but they do. And do you have that special place in your yard, the place with the stones or shrubs that mark where a good dog sleeps the sweet sleep, and do you go there to feel the sharp, nasal sting of tears...and remember?

If you do, then no matter where you live, you're a quail hunter, and this book is meant for you. You're one of a special breed.

STEVE SMITH
Traverse City, Michigan

Artist's Acknowledgements

I want to thank all of the generous property owners who have allowed me invaluable access to their farms, ranches, and plantations to gather the material I used to do the paintings and drawings for this book.

I also have to thank my fellow hunters who put up with so many photo interruptions on their days afield with me and my camera.

HERB BOOTH
Rockport, Texas

CHAPTER ONE

Meet the Gentleman Game Bird

by
Charley Dickey

THE BOBWHITE QUAIL is not named for a Southern gentleman named Bob White, but for the plaintive calls lonesome males make in spring and summer to any available female. Poets and gardening ladies romanticize the clarion signals of *"bob white," "bob, bob white"* or *"uh, bob white,"* but the males don't whistle just to entertain people.

They stake out a rough territory and signal other males to go find their own homesteads. They also whistle to attract cooperative hens, and any female will do. There's some question whether or not the hen is attracted to the male or to the territory he claims. If you think about it, things are about the same with humans. Have you ever heard of a millionaire who had trouble getting a date? Since there are more males than females during the mating season, it's no wonder the bobs do a lot of whistling. Who wouldn't? Nobody wants to get left out of recreational activities.

When a hen coyly approaches, it's love at first sight. The male doesn't worry if she's a blonde or brunette or has warts. She survived the winter, and that automatically means she's of legal age and there won't be any trouble about that. She's receptive, or she wouldn't have responded, and that's the main idea and gets things off to a good start.

If a bachelor male tries to invade the territory before or after the female arrives, the owner will defend his honor with a great deal of huffing, puffing, and a little wing-dragging. Sometimes there will be a bit of sparring, but there are no injuries other than to pride. The males don't want to kill one another; they just want to be left to breed in peace – we can all understand that. As a general rule, the male who first staked the territory wins, and the invader saunters off to try somewhere else – normal for many species of birds.

During the process of covey-breakup in spring, a pair may start sneaking off to enjoy the day together. They return at dusk to spend the night with the remnant covey, all roosting tail to tail in a circle, with heads outward for sudden departure.

Hunters worry about quail inbreeding more than the birds do. In fact, the birds hardly ever consider incest, and if they did, it wouldn't slow courtship. As the hours of increasing daylight passing into the eyes stimulate hormones, the quail just get down to the business of reproducing the species. Actually, the birds don't need legalities about incest; the coveys get bounced around during hunting season, there's a fall shuffle to find winter habitat, and males roam in the spring seeking breeding territory. Nature's dispersal laws pretty well take care of inbreeding. If a little harmless incest results in inferior young, predators or disease quickly cull them from the flock. That's a good system. I have never shot an inferior bobwhite. If I did, I wouldn't bring it up; there are places where the words "inferior" and "bobwhite" used together will get you punched in the face.

When a male and a female are struck with mutual affection, they get married for the season. If both survive until the following spring, each may choose another mate. It's a no-fault divorce and none of the quail get upset about it. Quail accept a little variety in mates and demand it in their habitat.

The males are loyal husbands, at least for the breeding and growing seasons. They help with the nest building, usually in fairly thick ground cover not far from an open area, such as a trail, woods road, or an edge. The male relieves the female from long hours of sitting on the eggs. As the brood grows, the male is almost as attentive to the young as the female. Most human wives would be happy to have a husband so devoted to the children's welfare. It's accepted behavior with quail, and the hen never has to nag her mate. But, there's evidence that the males are more polygamous than we used to think, servicing unattached hens that wander by.

The male and female are both shy about the actual sex act and don't like others watching. Even with pen-raised birds, where pairs are kept in caged layers, the birds are shy about breeding if they are not secluded. Most ardent quail hunters have never seen bobwhite copulating. Hunters don't really waste a lot of time worrying about it; they just want to know what the hatch in general is and where the birds are during the hunting season.

After the cock bird does his duty, the hen will lay about one egg a day. The average number of eggs in the Deep South is fourteen. After the last egg is dropped, the hen starts incubation, with the male hanging around as a relief clutch warmer. Incubation lasts twenty-three days, and then the tiny chicks begin pipping.

As the babies break through the delicate pale blue or pastel green shells, all sorts of weird things happen to the hen that cause false rumors to circulate among hunters. Rumors may turn into traditional beliefs, strong enough to precipitate a barroom brawl regardless of the season.

Once the chicks find freedom from their calcium cages, the nesting instincts of the hen are satisfied. She won't get romantic again until the following spring. As far as the male is concerned, she has a perpetual headache for several months.

The confusion among hunters arises because they see new clutches of young chicks from June until September or even October. What happens is that if a nest of eggs is destroyed before breakout, the reproductive instincts of the hen are not satisfied. She is willing and anxious to start the process all over again from scratch. The male is happy to oblige her.

If the second nest is destroyed before pipping, they will try a third, or even fourth time. They don't give up easily, which is a good thing for hunters and the survival of bobwhite quail. So, a summer observer may see new clutches from late spring into autumn.

Above all, a bobwhite quail is a social bird and feels sorry for orphans. If a male and female come across orphans from another pair, it doesn't take a TV appeal for them to adopt the foundlings. They just whistle, "Join our family. We're glad to have you." It's not unusual to see a hen with two or three different-aged groups in late summer. The logical conclusion is that the hen brought off more than one clutch, but logic and facts are two different things. Casual observers are not long on either one. Most hunters are not keen on reading technical biological reports, especially since a lot of them nurse a keen mistrust of wildlife biologists to begin with. Something grandpappy handed down, which sounds good, is more readily repeated than something a smart-assed, college-boy biologist proved.

In the early part of the hunting season, it is not unusual to flush a covey of ten-week-old birds, called "squealers" or "peepers." It takes about seventeen to nineteen weeks for the young of the year, or juveniles, to reach maturity or have close to full body weight and a plumage suitable enough for wildlife artists. On the other hand, birds seven days to two weeks old start taking short flights and quickly graduate to longer flights. They'd better, or they won't survive.

By the time quail are eight to ten weeks old, they have good body size and often flush as a unit. There is an instant temptation to shoot as the "squealers" flush, especially if you haven't had a shot for a couple of hours or since last season. When the juveniles fly, they call a shrill *"peep, peep, peep."* The true sportsman lowers his shotgun. He doesn't want to shoot young juveniles, but hopes to find them a few weeks later when they are mature. Any experienced hunter who knocks down a "squealer" immediately turns to his partner and says, "I thought it was a covey of hens" or "It was time I shot a bird for the dogs."

WHATEVER you think about the bobwhite's system of reproducing and perpetuating its species, there are good things and bad things. The best news is that the quail can take care of the multiplication and replenishing on its own. The Catch-22 is that he has to have the right habitat, not just during the hunting season, but every day of the year. No matter how adaptable the quail has become in the past forty years, he can't make it on a shopping mall's asphalt parking lot.

For any species of wildlife with a high reproductive potential, such as a pair of quail theoretically capable of multiplying themselves each year by a factor of seven times, there must be compensating factors. If you take out your pocket calculator, you can see that if one pair multiplies itself seven times one year, and the next year all of them increase by a factor of seven – well, it wouldn't take too long before we were all hip-deep in bobwhite quail. This still wouldn't be enough to satisfy some.

From the standpoint of the sportsman, the potential bounce-back of the quail population is a great thing. The fall population can be down one year, but it has the capability to bounce back the following year.

The trade-off with any species of wildlife with rapid duplication potential is that individuals usually don't live long. Nature is hard on the individual and mainly only cares about the survival of the species as a whole. In any given spring or summer replenishing season, most of the reproduction is done by birds born the year before.

Only twenty to thirty percent of the reproduction is done by two-year-old birds. The other two-year-olds would have liked to have been in on the action, but they died. A three-year-old quail in the wild is not a senior citizen, but closer to a fossil. It's a little different with protected pen-raised or pet quail; they don't have many hardships and may make it to four or five years. If you're wondering whether a two-year-old hen will mate with a one-year-old cock or vice-versa, the human equivalent of a seventy-year old marrying a twenty-year old, the answer is that birds don't worry about gossip. They just hop to it.

Quail in the wild cannot be stockpiled over any extended period. It's a high mortality of seventy to eighty percent in native bobwhite, regardless of hunters. If the hunters don't take the annual surplus, something else will. The classic example is Indiana and Ohio. For more than a half a century, the bunny-huggers in Ohio forced a closed quail season. The quail did not increase. Indiana, next door with roughly the same weather and habitat, allowed its hunters to enjoy quail hunting. The quail did not decrease, other than what could be attributed to changing land use.

Although the bobwhite is thought of as a cheery bird, it leads a hard life. Everything wants to eat it. Even before the birds are born, snakes, crows, raccoons, and other wildlife prey on the eggs. After it's born, it's a tempting morsel for any animal that can catch it – foxes, feral cats, certain species of hawks, coyotes, etc.

That's not to say you can manage quail by making war on

predators. The answer is to leave or develop enough protective cover for a fair percentage of the birds to breed, nest, and survive by escape or hiding.

Total predator control cannot be an economical answer, because the worst predator of all is man, but not the hunter. When quail populations dwindle during the hunting season, or there's a poor breeding season, the hunting pressure automatically decreases. When a hunter can't find enough birds to justify his efforts, he does the house chores his wife has been nagging him about for months, and there are enough birds left to replenish the habitat the following spring and summer.

It's the destruction of the habitat where humans wreak havoc on wildlife. If man's insecticides and pesticides don't directly kill the birds, some of them do indirectly by killing the insects and other food the quail require.

Give the quail a chance and they'll take care of themselves. If you're trying to manage quail, just remember that there are limitations. You can't stockpile quail and no matter how attractive you make the food and cover, the bird itself is a limiting factor. Millions of dollars have been lost on expensive quail plantations in South Carolina, Georgia, Alabama, and other states by not accepting the limitations. No matter how you diversify the cover and how many feed plots you plant, in a yearly cycle, the bobwhite quail will not be crowded beyond a certain point. If it will make you feel better, you can blame it on the chaos factor in physics.

As a general rule of quail management, if you can average one quail per acre over any extended time in the Old South, you are doing a pretty good job and can pat yourself on the back. Please don't write me any letters on quail population statistics. I've been on plantations where in a good year they might start the fall with two birds an acre average. I've also hunted an intensely managed plantation where biologists counted 2.8 birds per acre for *one* season, without mentioning their enticements to recruit coveys from adjoining farms. I recently hunted this same area with *their* dogs, and we worked hard to find six coveys all day.

Hunters believe what they want to believe. It doesn't necessarily coincide with what the quail do. That's okay. We all like to hear good stories.

When the tiny chick pips its escape exit from the restricting eggshell, it's a pitiful blob of limp moisture. For strength to meet its frightening new world, it has absorbed the remnants of its egg sac through the rectum. The mother hen, and perhaps to some degree its brothers and sisters, instinctively gives the baby bird comfort and security. As the chick dries, it is a helpless creature barely larger than a bumblebee.

NO hunter can watch a clutch of day-olds fleeing to the sanctuary of mother's protective wings and breast without a rush of emotion and wonderment. It's motherhood, apple pie, and flag-waving with a few ruffles of feathers as the hen snuggles her brood into protective custody. If the chicks were not already genetically wired to sociability, the early close association would get them there by another route. For the rest of their lives, they will never voluntarily be alone. In one way it's a strength, but it's a weakness when hunted. When the hunter finds one quail, he knows there are others nearby.

Dressed in its natal down, the day-old chick soon starts exploratory walks and tumbles, never far from the parents' legs and enveloping wings. He has to learn fast to seek protection and food. He's instinctively attracted to small, moving insects. They're his life's blood. He must have the protein; the chick is a meat eater. For rapid growth and body maintenance, at least thirty percent of his intake must be protein, about three times the maintenance level of a mature pointing dog.

The little ball of fuzz is a hunter. He gulps down nearly any

insect he can catch, taking no time to savor it but hastily searching for another. He also begins his lifetime habit of mixing in fresh greens – his salad, fiber, and one source of vitamin A and trace minerals. Very quickly he begins adding sand as an inner millstone to grind his food. Since he nearly doubles in size every week for the first eight weeks, he has to scramble hard to make a living. If his mother is killed, his father takes over full parental duties, which he has been sharing from the beginning.

A hunter cannot observe a delicate clutch of chicks without wondering, "How will those little brown and yellow shadows ever make it?"

Well, most of them won't. There are a dozen species of predators waiting to pounce. There is farm machinery, livestock, and speeding cars. There are internal and external parasites. Viruses and bacteria await for the bird to weaken. There are strong winds and cold rains. Nature did not *intend* for the whole clutch to survive, but only enough for the species to continue.

The superior and luckier chicks grow rapidly. At one week of age they make their first solo flights, not far, but enough to get their confidence up. They learn to scratch for bugs, although they keep an eye on the deeper cuts the hen makes. They learn to take moisture from the morning dew and to cleanse themselves in the dust. They note each type of cover from the low-lying grass where they can hide, to the briar thickets where some predators cannot follow them. They live in a hard world where one mistake may be their last.

Perhaps they feel the most secure of all when they cuddle up under their mother's warmth from some threat or to spend the night. As they become too large to huddle under her wings, they begin sleeping tail-to-tail in a circle. When cold weather comes, they may extend their wings to form a canopy which holds the heat of their bodies. No one leaves the circle to go to the bathroom. With a new roost, there will be a ring of droppings in the morning. If they continue to use the same spot, it will gradually fill in and become a black and white guano disc.

The average hunter walks with his eyes five-and-a-half feet or so above the ground. The bobwhite quail has a lower perspective, perhaps five or six inches with a straining neck. The quail wants its feet on the ground. The bird also wants to watch for danger as it feeds, rests, loafs, dusts, or plays. That means it wants open, bare, or sparse cover from its toes to higher than its head. The bird uses sunny spots when it's cold; also, much of its food is found where the sun can energize the ground plants.

The bobwhite quail is a bird of edges and small clearings and open woods, except when it's escaping. That's where it prefers to spend most of its daylight hours. Where the coveys are when you find them is a different matter. I have never seen a couple of hunters with a brace of pointing dogs capable of silently sneaking up on an unsuspecting covey. In fact, most quail parties couldn't sneak up on a deaf watchman in a steel foundry.

The birds may flush from dense wiregrass or broom sedge, but they ran in it to hide when they heard your party coming. When they first heard you, they were probably sifting sand and telling bawdy stories in the middle of a canopied sandy road. When you flush the covey, it will disperse to kudzu, honeysuckle, impenetrable pine stands, swamps, or worse. If you didn't shoot any birds, it will give you some satisfaction to know the birds don't like it in there. They will soon come out, probably after you're back home, so they can roost together. No bobwhite quail likes to sleep alone.

As autumn approaches, the juveniles will begin to eat more of summer's bounty, such as cereals, wild seeds, berries, and mast crops, pine seeds, and acorns. But right up until frost, the mature birds and juveniles don't miss a chance to snag a protein-laden bug or grasshopper.

One quail authority reported that across its range the bobwhite quail races ate at least two thousand different foods. I don't know if he included various species of insects, but it does show that the bob is an adaptable trencherman. The variety of food is not as critical as the fact that there be some food every day, especially during the cold, wet days of winter. If the bob's inner furnace can be stoked each day, especially with starches such as corn, it can survive some pretty rough weather. It is rare to open the crop of a quail in hand, even in late winter, that there aren't a few sprigs of green. Like all birds, the bob needs huge amounts of food because of his fast metabolism – a way of staying light, an adaptation for flight.

Hunters, and especially those who manage quail, are forever arguing over what *one* food is the favorite of bobwhite quail. That's about like fighting over the best ice cream at Howard Johnson's. It would be easier on Howard to stock only one flavor, but people change their minds. On top of that, palates change.

I suspect that quail are much like hunters in that both eat whatever is available. With hunters, there's usually a factor of who's going to buy and fix it. On a plush plantation, I once opened the crops of birds shot from four successive coveys in a fairly small area. One set had milo seeds, another was loaded with weed seeds, the third had mostly corn, and the fourth set was bulging with acorns. All had a small smattering of greens. Any covey having a hankering for the other food could have easily changed feeding areas.

If you have feed plots, don't be surprised if the birds fill up on wild partridge peas for a while. For feed strips or field feeders, it's a good idea to provide a variety, if it's economical. The critical time to help the birds is from January until green-up. By that time, some of the food will have rotted. The later it gets toward green-up, the more scarce the food. Hard seeds that don't rot, such as bicolor lespedeza, may not be eaten until February or March. As for food choices, I don't know if a quail prefers vanilla or chocolate, but if he gets hungry, he'll eat raspberry. You may want to ask the quail.

As autumn colors into fall, there is a shifting of the coveys to winter headquarters. It's called the "fall shuffle," and the coveys move a hundred yards to a few miles, the longer distances in arid country. Where there is ample dew and a few winter greens, the birds do not have to have running or standing water. Some coveys live all of their lives without seeing a branch or creek, even where the Army Corps of Engineers has not been there first.

During the shuffling and settling, an indefinite number of individuals switch coveys. At the start of the hunting season, a covey may have from eight to twenty birds, although ten to fourteen is more typical. Once in a while, a startled hunter may push up thirty birds. Usually that's a case of two coveys that happened to be feeding together.

WHEN not subject to undue pressure, a typical covey usually walks to a feeding area about an hour after daylight. They feed for an hour or two and then stroll back to a loafing area where they can loaf with their feet on the ground but with a low canopy of cover overhead or close by. They are seldom far from dense cover they can run or fly to quickly.

About two hours before dark, they make their second main feeding foray of the day. Just before dusk, they either fly or walk to a roosting spot, perhaps a new one but probably an old one if it has gone unmolested. For scattered bobwhites, their most plaintive recall or join-up calls are saved for the last hour before dark. The woods and dales ring with their urgent pleas of *"perlee"* or *"uh-perlee,"* roughly translated to mean "I'd rather sleep with a stranger than no one at all."

If a covey is bounced around a lot, it will change patterns. Instead of ambling to feeding areas at its regular times, it may fly to feed during the middle of the day. The birds quickly gorge until their crops are lopsided, and then fly back to dense

cover. There are no scent trails on the ground, and it's much harder for the dogs to find them.

If the weather is cold and rainy in the morning, a covey may stay huddled in bed. On windy days, the birds don't do as much ground-rambling, evidently because they don't hear danger as well and it's harder to see predators in the weaving grass and bobbing leaves and branches.

One study over 1,500-acre courses on prime plantation country, where the coveys were plotted before the hunting season, showed that hunters with a brace of dogs would, on the average, find about half of the coveys. On good days, they might find eighty percent of the coveys, but on the cold blustery days, maybe only twenty or thirty percent. The good days are the ones the hunters remember and talk about at the local ice cream parlor.

THE bobwhite quail during the past forty years has undergone a remarkable acceleration of evolution and adaptation to increased human pressure and changing land use. If it had not, it would have been on the list of threatened species.

Up to the thirties and World War II, the bobwhite was a bird of woodland edges and fed well out into grain or weedfields. The covey was predictable. When it flushed, a hunter with a broken arm had time to fire three shells and reload. That's when all of those stories about getting five birds on the covey rise got started. The singles only flew a hundred to two-hundred yards and sat down *in the open*. Anybody could mark them down. What's more, the dogs could too.

The singles mostly flew straight away, and it was not difficult for a pair of hunters to easily bag five or six. Even the missed singles didn't fly far into the woods and could be followed for another shot. What's more, the remnant covey stayed in its regular territory after the pounding. One of the sportsman's main conversation topics was how far down a covey should be shot before it was left alone. The only thing lower than an egg-sucking dog was a hunter who shot a covey into oblivion.

As a matter of survival, the bird was forced to change. Only the smart, adaptable quail survived until spring to reproduce and keep his genes going. "Smart" meant birds that preferred to run rather than hold for dogs, or if they did hold, to flush before the hunters loafed into shotgun range. Smart meant the grasscutters, the zippers, dipsy-doodlers, the hot-dogs, the speedsters, and the long fliers who wouldn't think of landing until they'd flown a half a mile, then they'd duck down, make a ninety-degree turn, and pick up some more distance. On much public land today, it doesn't pay to try to follow the singles – it's more efficient hunting to look for another covey.

By 1950, there were three times as many hunters as in the thirties. On top of that, there were more people rambling the outdoors than ever before (and that was before the hippies came along who lived out there). And if that wasn't enough to upset quail, most of their former habitat got torn up and converted into farm products, pine trees, pavement, and other progress, not to mention deadly pesticides and insecticides.

Only the most adaptable birds could survive. The low-fliers begat low-fliers. The swamp birds begat runners. The long-fliers begat aerobatists. The thicket-dwellers begat jumpy time changers. Every spring there was a whole lot of begatting going on, but only those with survival selections got in on the fun.

When the results of this evolution became evident in the 1960s, many sportsmen blamed it on the stocking of bobwhites from Mexico and Texas. Actually, there weren't enough Mexican quail released to make a dent in the gene pool, but they've come in handy for excuses. When a covey flushes wild today, a hundred yards ahead of the hunters, or runs to the swamps rather than holding for the dogs in the open, a hunter shouts, "Those

Mexican quail have done it to us again!"

The past decade, I have seen quail so far back in the Virginia woods that a self-respecting ruffed grouse wouldn't even visit his grandmother there. And I've seen Alabama coveys running into swamps so wet that the birds are probably evolving webs between their toes. I have a couple of males working my bird feeders each summer, and I live in the *middle* of a city.

How much more will the bobwhite change in the approaching years? As long as the bob makes it, I don't care. The hunter is looking for a challenge, isn't he? If it develops to the point I can't get within shotgun range, it's always a delight to hear his cheery "*bobwhite*" on a sunny spring morning.

CHAPTER TWO

Point, Flush, & Retrieve

by
James D. Nelson, M.D.

"POINT! OLD JOE'S GOT BIRDS UP AHEAD!"
Those words are the heartsong of the quail hunter. For just as "bird" means bobwhite, "Old Joe" or "Sweet Belle" are the heart of the hunting.

When the New Englander dreams of grouse shooting, he recalls the bright colors of the autumn forest. The Midwest pheasant hunter may envision a cackling rooster rising up over an unpicked cornfield. But quail hunters, whether they be Midwesterners, Texans, or good old boys from the Deep South, envision a tense, motionless pointing dog announcing the whereabouts of Gentleman Bob and friends.

In quail hunting, it is not the geographic area the birds are located, nor is it always a typical scenic setting that draws the hunter. In quail hunting, to me, the essence of the pursuit is between a dog and a bird; the hunter is there only to guide the dog from one promising place to the next.

Quail hunting without a dog is an exercise in futility. The quail is a friendly fellow and likes company, so he's initially difficult to locate. The bird's being a groupie instead of an independent means that a dog must quickly search a wide area to locate this congregation of birds known as a covey. Once located and subsequently flushed, a covey temporarily separates and becomes individual lost souls – singles. The scent given off by an entire covey of birds is greatly diminished when a lone bird escapes under layers of straw grass. It is then that a dog of caution and special scenting powers is needed to locate these singles. Once a quail is pointed, and occasionally downed, a persistent, ground-scenting retriever is an absolute must in order to find dead or crippled birds. These small birds, after being shot but not killed, can run with the best of wily pheasants. So, the "perfect" quail dog must have the skills of three dogs in one controllable package.

But just what *is* a good quail dog? He is a big, wide-ranging, hard-running, short-coated, white and liver dog with a cracking high tail. She is a miniature fine-boned, cautious, underfoot spaniel with no tail. It's a sleek no-nonsense Teutonic pointing machine that can hunt all day and retrieve birds with the tenacity and dash of a champion Lab. The dog is a dashing longhair of white, black and tan, or red that flows gracefully through thorny cover. As with many things in life, there are a number of ways to do a job well, and quail hunting is no exception: The four-legged characters are as varied as the two-legged ones puffing along behind them.

Quail dogs are either born or made. The really great ones are born with all of the search, point, and desire to please present in adequate amounts. Then, some lucky fellow who lives in Quail Haven, USA hunts this gifted dog four days a week from the time it's a nine-month-old pup. The good dogs either have some natural ability, such as a lot of pointing desire or a lot of drive to search, or else have a little talent but happen to do their hunting and learning in an area crawling with quail. The ones that don't live in quail country and are short of point, search, and pleasantries ought to stay at home.

In order to get your hands on a great quail dog, you can develop it from an early stage or buy it all ready to hunt. If you're going to take a chance on a puppy younger than nine months, then most of what you've bought is potential, and your decision will be based on genetics – parents and pedigrees. The younger the pup, the more emphasis the buyer is placing on the recombination of the sire and the dam's genes. So when buying a pup to be used for quail hunting, buy one from someone who hunts quail with his dog – and from an area that has an abundance of quail.

Developing a quail dog can be fun, time-consuming, and varies between frustration and ecstasy. How do you go about developing a good quail dog? This is the question that's probably moved you to read this chapter. Any breed of dog is more fun to hunt quail with than no dog.

TRADITIONALLY, upland gunners prefer pointing dogs for quail-field sport. In almost all instances, I like a pointing breed over a flushing spaniel for quail. Pointing dogs should search for quail and when the birds are located, the dogs should stop and indicate the bird's location by pointing, but not flushing. Most of us know how this routine works.

The gunners (in preference to the dogs) flush the birds and – arms flailing and eyes bugged out – attempt to shoot at the fleeing bumble bee-like targets. If the gunners get lucky and knock a few birds down, the scenting powers of the dog are called upon to find the dead or crippled birds and bring them to the gunners.

An important attribute that is often overlooked is that of backing or honoring another dog's point. A dog that will stop and point well behind a dog that has already located game and is pointing is a sight to behold. Quail hunting is supposed to

be fun. Over the years, I would say that most times when I wasn't enjoying myself, it was almost always because I was hunting with dogs that would not honor or back each other's points. I believe there are more strained friendships over a dog's failure to back than any other aspect of upland hunting. Some dogs that have a great deal of pointing instinct will back naturally. Others must be taught to "whoa" or stop behind another dog on point. In a lot of cases, this is the last lesson a bird dog is taught; any sportsman who has had a potentially great quail hunt ruined by dogs that won't honor would probably suggest that it be first.

I've talked with several older trainers of the past who did, indeed, start a pointing dog's training with honoring. One long-time trainer of gun dogs from Nebraska said he always "let the old bitch train her own pups." He explained that after planting a bird, he would let the old bitch find and point it. Then he would bring out the pup who would, of course, follow mom. He said occasionally he would be able to stack up an entire litter behind the old bitch by the time they were twelve weeks old.

The most common method of teaching a dog to back is probably that of whoa-breaking a dog – teaching it to stop and remain motionless when the command "whoa" is issued. An older, completely staunch dog is allowed to find and point a bird. Then, a youngster who has previously been instructed in the fine art of honoring is brought up at a distance of several yards behind the first dog. This particular procedure can be a snap for breeds that like to point. However, breeds in which the retrieving instinct is dominant often are not good backing candidates because they want to be as close as possible to the flush in order to make the retrieve.

The two best dogs I've owned were a huge, slow German shorthair bitch by the name of Bridget, and a dynamic walking-shooting dog Irish setter field champion – Big Al. Over the years, Bridget had become one of the greatest singles dogs I've ever seen. She would point every single after the covey was scattered and could mark and retrieve four birds on a covey rise while her bracemate would come up empty-handed. A perfect dog you ask? Nope! She did not comprehend or else would not tolerate "whoa." I set her back, thumped on her, roped her, whoaed her, and I even used the most damnable of all training tools: the shock collar. When I finally resorted to the collar, the hair on her back stood up in a two-inch band from the root of her tail to the back of her stubborn, German skull – while she crept toward the dog on point ahead of her. I mean, I lit her up like a Christmas tree. Nothing.

She never backed a dog in her life until she met the debonair fellow from Ireland. Somehow, they worked out a pact between them. Big Al would almost always find and point the covey, often two-hundred yards in front of Bridget, and Bridget would "honor." I would hustle up there and shoot what I could. Bridget would retrieve the birds, Al would go find another covey, and Bridget and I would go point and shoot a few of the singles. It was a great combination – a lifelong dream, the ultimate short dog and the ranging covey-finder. Al was a great singles dog and an excellent retriever, but in those years that I hunted them together he was a true gentleman, allowing Bridget to make the retrieve and point more than her share of the singles and, in turn, that huge stubborn bitch didn't break his covey finds.

The final aspect that determines the success of the quail team – dog and man – is that of handling. A dog that handles just plain makes for a pleasant day afield. In this age of closer-working Continental dogs, it is often assumed that Brits, shorthairs, Weimaraners, and wirehairs handle, and pointers and setters don't. In other words, the range of the dog is a determinant factor in how cooperative the quail dog is to the master. Naturally, a Weimaraner hunting at thirty yards certainly appears to be easier to handle than a streaking

pointer at a quarter of a mile. My own belief is that the actual relationship that exists between the hunter and the dog determines handling qualities. A dog of restricted range is in close contact with the gunner and, therefore, is subjected to the potential for more handling – whistling, shouting, or merely the reassurance of the gunner's presence. However, I believe that the true test of a handler lies in his ability to guide a wide-ranging dog that seeks objectives and is not always within voice range.

A covey-seeking pointer at two-hundred yards that glances back over his shoulder as he approaches the crest of a hill is one to make you proud. I believe it takes a greater investment in time to instill this constant presence in a wide-ranging dog – an amount of time and energy that a lot of hunters are not willing to spend.

If a person is going to start with a puppy from proven quail-dog genetics, several good books such as those written by Ken Roebuck, John Falk, and Dave Duffey will provide the basics for starting a young pup. Pointing, retrieving, and how to teach your dog to whoa are all covered by these very knowledgeable author-trainers. But handling a dog is an art. It seems that years of experience are necessary to develop first-rate handling capabilities.

The term "handling" is often applied to the four-legged portion of the quail hunting team when, in reality, this term is usually a trait exhibited or overlooked in the dog owner. When I get an eight-week-old pup of any breed, the first thing I consider is how I'm going to handle this particular dog. If the dog is aggressive or is from a strain or breed of dogs known to be aggressive, I may be a bit heavy-handed, even at this young age.

With any dog that I want to be close-working, or with a big-running dog that I want to be responsive to my presence, I simply get lost. The way I go about this is to take the pup out for a walk in moderately thick cover (after a week or two of

getting acquainted). Once the pup has moved out away from me and is busy snooping around or chasing butterflies, leaves, or his shadow, I very discreetly hide by lying down out of sight from young Quail Buster. After a bit, the pup finds that I'm not around. Since he's becoming attached to me and, in fact, I've become his mother, the pup becomes quite concerned. I've seen pups search frantically or sit down and howl pitifully. Once the pup finds me, he's usually so happy that he stays close. If this process is repeated a couple of times at an early age, I've found that even the most aggressive pups from the boldest breeds never forget the lesson.

ANOTHER one of my thoughts about quail dogs concerns that of retrieving. I think we all would rather not shoot a bird than to shoot one and leave it in the field. I believe we have a duty to retrieve every bird we kill or cripple, and I feel the retrieve is as important as the point that located the bird in the first place. In the early years, some of the classic pointers and setters were not expected or allowed to retrieve downed quail. Happily, retrieving is now in vogue for all bird dogs. Some purist may still claim that in order to keep his pointing dog staunch, he prefers to not allow his dog to retrieve. To this very proper gentleman, I would recommend the age-old tradition still carried on in the grouse moors of Scotland and in the Deep South where plantation-style hunting still exists. In both these areas, the classic pointing breed – pointers and setters – initially locate the birds by pointing. The gunners arrive on the scene, shoot, the pointers are sent on to locate more game, and handlers bring in either spaniels or one of the standard retrieving breeds to find and bring to hand the downed birds.

As I dream of quail hunting, I envision a staunch, rippling orange-and-white pointer, high at both ends, pointing a covey of birds in broom grass sprinkled with pine trees. This scene always occurs in the South, and it's a classic. If the truth be known, the typical scenario for me is an old, whitefaced, tired Irish setter pointing with a straight, out-the-back tail full of burrs along a fenceline bordering a milo field in the Midwest. The reality of the situation is that a pointer looks great in our dream world, but would probably freeze to death in the Great American Icebox in January.

A breed of dog that produces birds in south Texas is not necessarily the answer in southwest Iowa. The quail lives and thrives in huntable numbers in a huge part of this country. Due to the varying weather conditions and topography encountered over these areas, it's impossible to conventionalize the present-day quail dog.

In certain areas of the country, only coveys are sought and covey rises are where the birds are bagged or missed. In other areas of the country, gunners shoot over covey points, but singles shooting is the bread and butter. The breed or individual dog that a sportsman chooses to gun over should be determined by whether a covey or singles dog will be most useful under the conditions he hunts. Here, the term "conditions" is widely applied.

In the past, certain sections of the United States were noted for being breed-specific bird dog areas. As I began to hunt quail over a large portion of the United States, I started to have a better understanding of just why. The upper Midwest was traditionally an area of setters, English setters, of course, being more common, followed by sprinklings of Irish and Gordon. Along with setters were large-boned Britts. The Midwest had a smattering of various other breeds; one that certainly gained a strong following early on was the German shorthair.

Conditions to consider in choosing a breed are the topography of the land, the weather in which you hunt, the ground cover, and the size of tracts you hunt. Wide open, flat areas with few trees mean far-ranging dogs. Thick, brushy areas lend themselves to a close-working dog. A moist climate allows for the scenting conditions to be optimum and a

seeking, hard-driving dog works well. On the other hand, dry or sub-freezing weather conditions that inhibit scenting are best handled by a slower, more cautious dog. Grassy areas and warmer, sunny locations are best handled by light-coated, far reaching, horizon-type dogs. However, briars and extremely cold weather are better tolerated by heavy-coated bird dogs with restricted range.

English Pointer

The South, where warm weather abounds, has traditionally been pointer and, to a lesser extent, setter country. Down there the traditional long-tailed, covey-seeking breeds were right at home on some of the plantations and large paper company forest tracts. And then there is south Texas, where an old trainer from Houston once told me: "Everything either sticks, pricks, or bites you." In south Texas, the English pointer is about the only breed. That was one place Big Al, my aforementioned Irish setter, wasn't very big. Big Al was too dark red, which meant he soaked up heat like a sponge soaks water. And even though Big Al was a big-running dog for the Midwest, he couldn't hold a candle to even the medium-running dogs on their home turf. Pointers are, of course, scattered throughout the United States. But, these two areas are pointer strongholds.

The English pointer possesses more search than any other breed of bird dog. His single-mindedness in pursuit of birds is awesome, and his pointing instincts are second to none. A pointer will hunt with or for almost any handler and adapt to new areas with little difficulty.

The pointer hunts at a fast pace and usually relies on air scent to locate birds. Most pointers are more in tune to coveys than singles, although I've seen some excellent exceptions. If objectives on the horizon are where the quail are, then the English pointer is the fellow for the job. Due to his ambitious approach to finding birds, the pointer does his best work when conditions are right. Aggressiveness is his best asset, but in certain circumstances it can be his greatest liability. At optimum temperature, a mild breeze, and a little moisture, he is dynamite with his fast-paced approach.

However, when one or two of these factors are altered, the speed at which the pointer hunts may become a liability. In dry, dusty conditions, the pointer's speed may result in his bypassing single birds. English pointers are not usually overly affectionate, and I believe they function well in a kennel, so they easily transfer from one owner-handler to another.

The English pointer possesses a great amount of pointing instinct and, therefore, readily backs another dog's initial bird contact. In the past, pointers were neither expected nor allowed to retrieve, but recently shooters have found that English pointers can be extremely effective retrievers.

So, if you live in an area where a big running, hard-going dog is needed to find birds, the traditional choice of an English pointer is still viable. In fact, he is better today than he was in years past.

English Setter

The English setter is the classiest animal that hunts quail. A feather-white setter flowing through the cover is style personified. The classic poses he portrays on point, with his plume tail alerting God and gunner alike that here lies Bobwhite, will take a sportsman's breath away. The high-tailed, stylish English setter exudes beauty, grace, and style.

The setter we refer to as English is one of the most popular pointing dogs in the entire world. He may not rule certain areas of the country as the pointer does, but he has a huge following scattered over the entire United States. His outstanding beauty and style coupled with his typical easy-going, affectionate disposition endear him to a great many sportsmen.

The setter fancier is typically a patient fellow. Where the English and German pointers often are handling wild birds by their first year, the setter will often require two and one-half to three years to accomplish the same thing. The soft, brown eyes and the affable disposition makes it easy for the upland hunter who starts with a pup to weather the extra time necessary for a setter to mature.

There are a few distinct types of dogs within the English setter breed. These range from those ultra-fast coyotes of thirty-five pounds that almost fly, to seventy-five pound, sculptured, slow-working, walking-style dogs. Llewellin, Bondhu, Ryman, and Hemlock all refer to specific types of English setter popularized by individual breeders. Each one has type-specific tendencies in size and conformation, style on point, personality, ground race, and range. When you get ready to pick out your next pup, it is necessary to inquire as to the dog's genetic makeup and to specifics pertaining to both the dam and the sire. As stated earlier, when and if you are interested in purchasing any pup, make certain of its genetic background and the range, style, and traits of its parents. On the other hand, throw chromosomes to the wind when it comes to choosing a trained dog; then, rely on a demonstration and your own personal observations.

In my experience, the English setter has a great deal of pointing instinct. I've also been amazed at his scenting capabilities. Some of the longest noses I've run across have been attached to English setters.

When training any breed of setters, I don't try to teach the dog to do a particular task in a matter of minutes; I show him what I'd like him to accomplish and with repeated exposure, he seems to gather this information, sort it out, and put it together on his own time schedule.

I've heard a lot of quail gunners, especially those who spend a lot of time in the thickest stuff, say, "I'd sure like to try a setter, but I don't want to spend a lot of time cleaning up his coat." Often times some cleanup is necessary at the end of an early season day. However, this same problem coat also has some benefits. For a few years I hunted southern Georgia: Briarpatch, USA. I noted that parcels of cover packed with briar were often skirted by the slick-coated pointers. However, time and again the long-haired setter breeds charged through the meanest patches around unscathed.

The upland gunner who fancies setters must be willing to invest a great deal of personal time with his dog. Setters thrive on attention, so their best trainers are usually their masters. A setter is slower to mature, and those first two months of intensive bird training may be delayed until fourteen to eighteen months. The tradeoff for this, though, is that he often will hunt two to four years longer than those breeds that mature early.

If you want the most from a setter, move him into your life. This could be said of almost all the hunting breeds, but this one does the best of all in close relationships with family members. That's why setter owners seem to always be picking white hair off their blue suits – the dog probably sleeps on the good furniture, begs from the table, and generally makes himself right at home, thank you. At least the good ones seem to have worked out that kind of deal.

Brittany Spaniel

Now, about one of the most popular breeds: the Brittany spaniel. My first-ever, real-live bird dog was a Britt. Rusty was a tad kennel-shy, but we put some things together over a few months, and eventually he worked his way out of his shell. I was new at the pointing-dog game, and I even attended some field trials. In his second outing at one of these, Rusty found and pointed four birds in the bird field, and I was able to flush them all. Could have shot them, too – good finds. One shorthair pointed two birds, but no other dog nailed more than one. When Rusty placed fourth, I felt my eyes glaze over. An old-timer told me that even in the puppy stakes, the dogs that ran over the hill and had to be chased down and picked up at the end of the trial were looked upon favorably over my well-mannered buddy with the windshield-wiper tail. I thought the judges and handlers were a little confused, back then; now, twenty years later, I'm damned certain they were.

The Brittany, a pointing spaniel, originated as a poacher's dog in that part of France that gives the breed its name. He was bred to stay close to his handler (the poacher), point his game, and retrieve it after the shot. His diminutive size made him cheap to feed and easy to hide from the landowner's gamekeepers. His close race enabled the poacher to go about his nefarious activities free from the attention a wider-running dog would attract.

There are still some close-working Britts out there, but there are just as many that have been bred to run the all-age stakes against the long-tailed dogs – real smokers. Hence, the adage, "Let the buyer beware" especially applies when choosing a Britt. Check the pup's immediate background, and if you are purchasing a trained or started dog, try to get a look at him in action in cover familiar to him.

The Britt's small size makes him handy to house right alongside your wife and kids, neither of whom ends up as well trained or behaved. The Britt is often shy and reserved unless he is on familiar turf with people he knows and trusts. Most Britts would prefer the house to even a co-ed outdoor kennel. A Britt is a lot like a setter: You kind of let him set his own pace. In training a Britt, you show the dog what you expect and do this at opportune times until he decides this is what he wants to do. Pointing, retrieving, backing, and adjusting his range all come naturally to well-bred Brittanies.

Some may look at the Britt and dismiss him because of his

small size. However, this small size lends itself well to a particular type of quail hunting – singles. As he cautiously sniffs his way through the cover, his naturally low (in relationship to the ground) head position places him right down there where he needs to be to identify and point single quail.

Rusty was one of the best "dead bird" dogs I've ever seen. You knocked one down, and the only way to leave without picking up the dead bird was to chase the dog down and literally carry him from the area.

I've often thought that a Brittany is a reasonable, responsible sort of hunting companion. He seems to grasp the general idea of the hunt. I remember a snowy day when Rusty was pointing each and every single of a scattered covey. After he had pointed about six singles in a row that were all missed clean, Rusty took things into his own hands. The next three birds he pointed were all brought to hand. After establishing a point, waiting for us to trundle into position, adjust our caps, and get ready for the flush, he'd merely reach in, gently grab the quail, and deliver it to me. Some days, the dog just insists on doing the shooting.

Any long-tailed breed fancier that has no use for "those little French dogs" ought to see them vacuum up a covey of scattered singles, watch a Britt retrieve a dead quail from a fast river, or belly crawl and point his way through a log pile that a pointer or setter can't get under or go over.

Due to his small size, easily adaptable nature, great nose, determination, and hs own brand of style, the Brittany is the fastest-growing breed of pointing dogs in the country today. I predict that within a few years, he will overtake even the English setter.

German Shorthair

If I had to choose one dog to serve all of my hunting needs, there's no doubt in my mind what I would choose: a male German shorthair – male because I wouldn't want a three-week heat cycle to interfere with a long awaited quail trip to the South.

The shorthair originally established itself in the central and Midwestern areas of the United States. From the onset, here was a large rugged dog that could handle those cagey running pheasants with more finesse than any other pointing breed. Initially, the shorthair didn't attract too much attention from quail hunters because he was a very close worker. The quail hunter of the 1930s would have considered the shorthair a plodder. The German shorthair handled pheasants by establishing point and then relocating using air or ground scent to creep forward and then point again. Long ago, the quail hunter had no need for a plodder and a creeper because Gentleman Bob stayed put and didn't run off like his flashy colored, large northern cousin.

The quail hunter of the past was blessed with an abundance of birds. In the Deep South, spaniels and retrievers were often at heel to pick up the shot birds, a job the shorthair relishes.

Today's educated quail require different hunting methods. Today, quail stay in the heavy cover a greater portion of the day. Flushed quail have pre-planned routes of escape to extremely heavy cover that is nearly impossible to penetrate. And they *run*.

Now it is not uncommon to have an experienced quail dog point, creep, and point repeatedly until a covey is flushed. The singles dig in so deep that a good dog slows to a crawl in order to find and point the scattered birds.

Lately, quail hunting reminds the well-traveled upland gunner of pheasant or ruffed grouse hunting. The type of dog that will point and relocate moving birds is suddenly a desirable quail dog. The number of birds located in a day's shooting is fewer, and the number of acres available to the quail hunter is diminishing each season. With smaller daily bags, each and every quail shot is a trophy, and today's sportsmen demand a dog that retrieves – the plodder has come of age.

For a number of reasons, the German shorthair is the most popular of the dogs once considered boot lickers by the pointer-setter fanciers of yesteryear. The shorthair was one of the first of the Continental breeds to be established in numbers large enough to develop a good gene pool. He also has a short coat that endears him to some of us lazy, "don't like picking burrs," fellows. This short coat – still dense enough to protect him in icy water – enables him to adjust to the warmer climates of the South.

When studying the German shorthair, some prevalent characteristics are evident. The conformation retains some of the hound characteristics that are prevalent in his genealogy: long ears, soft eyes, and a body that sits well up on long, powerful legs. His heavy chest and hip structure project strength and endurance. The hound background is responsible for the breed's ability to put his nose to the ground and follow running or crippled birds.

The shorthair can develop a close relationship with "his family." Most of the shorthairs I've encountered make poor kennel dogs and fine house pets. After maturation is reached, they are reserved and graceful about the house. Always present but never a nuisance, unlike all setters and most Britts that regularly expect to sleep in your bed with you. They are extremely intelligent, and there is no limit to the amount of obedience training they readily absorb.

The breed has been around long enough to establish three varieties. One type is bred for appearance, but still retains some original hunting tendencies. The second is a variety that has been bred to run and seek over a far greater amount of ground than the original edition of sixty years ago. It is thought that this may have been accomplished with outcrossings to standard pointers. This smaller, quicker dog is valuable in locating coveys of birds in states where large parcels of land still exist. The last variety is from the type of dog originally imported from Germany, a large, close-quartering type of personal hunting dog that retrieves naturally. This type is currently showing up more frequently on quail-shooting preserves throughout the United States where a close-working dog that can point and retrieve is invaluable.

The German shorthair will continue to grow in popularity across the United States with quail hunters and all other upland sportsmen due to his natural traits, exceptional intelligence, and adaptability.

Weimaraner

The Weimaraner from Germany – with ghostly eyes that seem to read your soul. Originally, he was one of the do-it-all imports; this large, calm, happy fellow is now touted as a close-working pointing dog that has excellent retrieving habits.

The Weimaraners I've had the good fortune to hunt behind have all been slow, cautious, thorough hunters that possessed superior noses. Like the shorthairs, these guys will use both air scent and ground scent to locate and point birds. The average Weimaraner is larger, more heavily built, and slower than the German shorthair; he's also a one-man dog and therefore hunts strictly for his owner. For this reason, he is not a good choice for a preserve to own and expect to send out with other people. I've had a couple of Weimaraners that could handle singles with the finest of any breed. One of the things I've noticed with Weimaraners is a natural tendency to honor another dog's point. It would appear to me that he is a little stronger on backing than most of the other Continental pointing breeds.

The Weimaraner, due to his large size, matures both physically and mentally at a slower rate, and he approaches the setters in the length of time he takes to develop into a finished performer. The Weimaraner's coat is not extremely heavy and easily adjusts to the warmer sections of quail range.

Wirehaired Pointing Griffon

I like this fuzzy guy. The Griffon is an extremely animated, pleasurable hunting companion. Like the other Continentals, he has a slow, methodical pace. He works great in heavy cover and colder climates because his wiry outer coat protects him.

The Griffon moves easily despite his large size. He is an excellent retriever and the northern edge of the quail belt, where the temperatures often plunge below zero, is his home turf.

The Grif tends to be family oriented and, like a lot of the imports, works only for his master.

German Wirehair – Drahthaar

The wirehair is currently on a surge of popularity across a wide range of the United States. He is very similar in quite a few ways to his German shorthair cousin.

On the whole, the wirehair has a close quartering ground pattern. He will use both air scent and ground scent in locating his birds, and he is a natural retriever.

His coat offers great protection from cover that sticks and pricks and, of course, it protects him from the cold. The wirehair is an excellent singles dog. He is exceptionally calm and very intelligent. He travels easily and is a good choice for the Midwest quail/pheasant hunter.

Vizsla

The Vizsla is one of the more recent breeds to make inroads into the United States. He has a beautiful reddish-gold coat of short hair; evidently, extremely cold weather is not common on the Hungarian plains where this breed originated.

The Vizslas I've trained and hunted were superb. Using both air and occasionally ground scent, they possess excellent noses, exhibit a great amount of pointing instinct, and are natural retrievers. In fact, most of them have practically trained themselves. I found them extremely willing to please, and their natural abilities seem endless. Most of them are a pleasure to develop from a puppy.

Gordon Setter

This black and tan setter is one of the most attractive hunting dogs available in the United States. The Gordon is a slower-moving setter than his white and red cousins. Twenty years ago, the Gordon was a rare breed; today, he's definitely on the comeback trail. The Gordons I've hunted with rely on air scent. Most of them retrieve as well as the Continental breeds.

The Gordon is a people-oriented dog, and it is unusual for him to perform for anyone other than his master. The Gordon will air scent at a slower pace and, therefore, has a reputation of being extremely thorough in locating birds that other breeds might miss. I would consider a Gordon for a cold environment where his heavy black coat would be advantageous. He should also be at home in a dry climate where his slower pace would identify singles a faster-moving dog would miss. In the past, the age-old criticism of the Gordon setter was that his black coat made him difficult to locate. In today's hunting situations where the amount of cover is in short supply and less emphasis is placed on run and more on handling, black and tan works just fine.

Irish Setter

This jovial red fellow is alive, well, and hunting quail across the United States with typical Irish enthusiasm.

Thought by many sportsmen to be a breed of the past, the Irishman has actually made a welcome comeback over the past thirty years. As with most breeds today, the Irish or red setters are available in three distinct varieties: the red setter, a smaller, very fast, stylish field trial-type dog that proponents are now contesting against the long-tailed white dogs in field trials; the large, heavy boned, feathery coated show dogs that have not been bred with hunting desire or traits taken into consideration; and last, a field dog similar to that your great-grandfather hunted over at the turn of the century. This original Irish was the first dual-purpose dog in the United States, before we heard the term "Continental pointing breeds."

The Irish setter, probably enjoying his youth, develops slowly, often taking two to three years to get around to the very serious business of birds. However, the Irish setter lives longer than any other breed of pointing dog and often hunts into his teens.

The Irish, of course, has a darker red coat that in some instances has a harsh outer coat and a dense under coat. This is an advantage in colder climates, where he is at home, and areas where the foliage is constantly tearing at the dog's hide.

One advantage I've watched with Irish setters is their ability to penetrate heavy cover and cover full of thorns. In south Georgia where everything not a sidewalk is a briar patch, I've watched English pointers and some English setters tiptoe along the outside of the briars, only to have an Irishman charge through them like wheat stubble.

It may be hard to get an objective opinion from me about Big Red. As my wife would explain, "Doc has spent twenty years of wages, tears, and laughter on the Irishman." If you read a lot of gibberish by fellows who write on pointing dogs, someone always says his first dog or his best dog was an Irish setter. Well, here we go again!

"Big Al" inherited me when I was thirty-one and he was

four. He took great care of me for eight years. He led me to every out-of-the-way airport in twenty states chasing every species of quail on the continent, and slept in my overstuffed office chair while I struggled to gather together enough cash for our next excursion. He slept beside my bed and ate ice cream in the front seat of my brand new car. He was my best friend and I belonged to him.

And yes, Al was the greatest quail dog I've ever hunted with. He was the only dog I've ever seen that you would describe as both a great covey dog and a great singles dog. He never ran any faster than all of the white dogs, and he wasn't quite as thorough as the smallest Brittany bitch, nor would he slow down as much as the slowest German shorthair. He never flat out ran anyplace, but he always managed to get to the right place – where the birds were – a couple of minutes before any of the other dogs.

An Irish setter is certainly not for everyone, but if you are patient, enjoy a companion that has character, and like the type of dog that has a pace and heart that never quit, you might consider one of those jovial fellows from the Emerald Isle.

For those of us who think that quail hunting is nothing without the dogs – and I'd guess we all can agree on that – the call of the quail comes through loud and clear in the whine of a bird dog when he sees the gun, and the first, trembling point of a new pup.

Through training, conditioning, feeding, and just living with our dogs, we can make quail season last all year.

Morning Shooting
Courtesy of Meredith Long & Co.
Houston, Texas

Oakridge Covey
Courtesy of Meredith Long & Co.
Houston, Texas

Bracketed

Courtesy of Mr. Mike Hanson
Houston, Texas

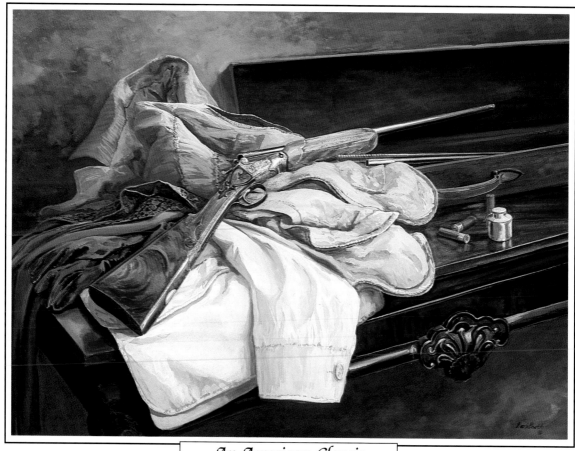

An American Classic

Courtesy of Meredith Long & Co.
Houston, Texas

Prairie Covey
Courtesy of Meredith Long & Co.
Houston, Texas

Windmill Covey

Courtesy of Mr. George Baker
New York, New York

Plantation Quail
From The North American Wingshooting Portfolio
Countrysport Press

CHAPTER THREE

Quail Gunning

by
Michael McIntosh

NEVER BET MONEY in a head-to-head quail shoot against a man who wears a canvas coat that looks like a hand-me-down from Nimrod's great-uncle and who carries a 20-gauge Model 12 that has all the blueing worn away and no front sight. Not that the coat matters much one way or the other; it's just part of the identifying plumage. The gun matters. Don't even bet that you can get off the first shot or even the second, because when a covey goes up, he'll shuck off three shells so fast that it'll sound like a chainsaw. If there aren't three birds for the dog to pick up, he won't make any excuses and he won't get upset – but there'll be three down the next time.

If you meet that man, take a half-hitch in your ego, keep your money in your pocket, and pay attention. You're about to see a natural at work.

You can ask him about his gun, but you won't learn much. He'll tell you that he's had it a long time and that it works okay. The fact is, he could take your gun and shoot just as many birds just as neatly, an equation that won't hold the other way around.

Everybody knows somebody who is a natural wingshot, and we all secretly wish we had whatever it is that sets the natural shot apart from the rest of us. And most of us would use that special gift, if we had it, to become quail shots in the stature of legend, because of all the birds there are to shoot, the measure of skill against bobwhite comes closest to accounting for the measure of the man.

Obviously, you can't *become* a natural quail shot, but it seems to me that anyone sufficiently coordinated to shave and blink at the same time can, with some practice and some experience, become a good quail shot.

That's my conviction, anyway, though I don't know whether I'm living proof or living refutation. I have no interest in keeping track of such things, but if I compared cartridges expended against birds in the bag, my shooting average at quail probably would be the poorest among all the birds I hunt – a repertoire that includes grouse, woodcock, pheasant, dove, ducks, pigeons, and several thousand clay targets every year.

In thirty years of trying to figure out why, I've reached a few conclusions, the most fundamental of which is that *the gun matters*. I can break a respectable number of skeet targets with almost any gun, mostly because I know where they come from, where they're going, and how long they'll take to get there. I can do much the same with pheasant and doves and ducks, but it doesn't work with quail. So the gun matters. And not just any gun will do.

Of all the criteria that define a quail gun, the least important is gauge. Twenty-bores are popular quail guns, but so are 12s, 16s, 28s, and even .410s. I've shot quail (and missed quail) with every one of them, and they all rendered well-hit birds equally dead. On the other hand, the cripples were cripples regardless of how large or small the offending barrel happened to be.

What the nature of quail shooting demands is a dense pattern of small shot delivered with minimal stringing. The only bore that doesn't qualify in that regard is the .410; the half-ounce skeet load doesn't hold enough shot to offer any reliable reach or any margin for error, and the three-inch version strings its shot so badly that you can throw a cocker spaniel through the pattern. Four-tens are better left to the naturals. Which gauge you choose among the others, though, doesn't matter. The gun matters.

What makes the 20-bore the be-all and end-all for so many quail shooters hasn't anything to do with the gauge's cartridge, but has a lot to do with the 20-gauge gun. Most American guns, for a number of reasons, are overbuilt and therefore heavy, which is true of doubles as well as pumps and autoloaders. Quail are small birds that don't require heavy loads, but they often do require a lot of walking. So, if you do your quail hunting from the comfort of a democrat wagon, you're apt to choose a lightweight gun because that's all you need; if you go after them afoot, you take a lightweight gun because a heavy one is torturous to lug around all day.

Either way, it usually boils down to a 20-gauge, because a 20 usually is the best compromise that American guns have to offer – not because there's anything magic about a .615-inch bore or ⅞-ounce of shot. The typical American 12-gauge, whether it was built in 1910 or last year, is likely to weigh well over seven pounds, which is more than enough to dampen the recoil of a light load and certainly more than enough to carry comfortably for very long.

Some of the old American doubles will give you a break on weight. A.H. Fox guns tend to be lighter, gauge for gauge, than the others. My pet 12-bore Fox weighs 6¾ pounds, and almost everyone who holds it remarks on how light it feels. You can find Fox 20s that weigh little more than five pounds. Ithaca and L.C. Smith made some lightweight pieces, too.

Parkers tend to be the heaviest of all, in any gauge.

Some of the old 16s, built in the days when gunmakers put 16-gauge barrels on real 16-gauge frames, are delightful guns for any upland game, but finding 16-gauge cartridges suited to quail instead of rhino can be a chore. Anything more than $2\frac{1}{2}$-dram equivalent loads behind an ounce of shot is unnecessary in a 16, either for a quail or for the shoulder behind the gun.

In any case, the situation among American guns is that finding less weight almost always means accepting a smaller bore as well. There certainly is nothing wrong with small-bore guns, so long as you don't feed them more shot than they can handle efficiently; but the great law of shotgun ballistics is that the larger the bore relative to the shot charge, the more efficient performance becomes.

The guiding principle among European makers, alien though it is to the American industry, is that guns are specialized tools, tailored to a certain maximum load. For the typical game gun, that amounts to an ounce or at most $1\frac{1}{8}$ ounces of shot. An ounce of shot through a 12-gauge barrel is an uplander's dream, and if you browse among the best English and Italian and French and Spanish guns, you'll find lots of 12-bores built for just that load. They'll weigh about six pounds or a bit more, and if you shoot one for a while, you'll never want to use anything else.

Naturally, they'll beat the hell out of you if you give them heavy loads, but an uplander doesn't need heavy loads in any gauge. My favorite game load for everything but ducks is an ounce of hard shot in a 12-gauge cartridge, and it's equally effective for doves, pheasants, and birds of all sizes in between. If you're a handloader, there are some excellent recipes for $\frac{7}{8}$-ounce 12-gauge loads, and they shine, too. I shoot a zillion of them every year at skeet. They'll smoke a clay target from any station and do the same thing to a game bird anywhere inside forty yards or thereabouts.

A few blatherskites insist that shooting a quail with a 12-gauge is somehow unsporting. None that I've talked with has ever been able to tell me how an ounce of shot from my 12 is any less sporting than the same ounce from his 20. The most I've learned from those people is that their concept of sportsmanship is starkly different from mine. Sportsmanship is one case where the gun really doesn't matter. Sportsmanship, to my mind, lies in the decision to shoot or not to shoot at a given animal, and if I decide to shoot, I want that animal dead as cleanly and efficiently as possible. I see nothing sporting about using a load so inefficient that the odds of crippling are higher than those of a clean kill. Nor do I see any sense in overloading a small gun to the point that I'm too busy flinching from recoil to shoot well.

So, if you have a good 12-gauge game gun and want to shoot quail with it, there's no reason in the world why you shouldn't. Likewise a 16, a 20, or a 28. Gauge doesn't matter.

Weight does matter, though, and how that weight is distributed matters even more. A quail gun needs to be light enough to carry without becoming burdensome, but this isn't to say that a four-pound gun is necessarily better than one that weighs six pounds or even seven. You might be a quail-shooting whiz with a four-pound gun, but I couldn't shoot one worth a damn, especially at quail. A quail gun is one that strikes the optimal balance in accommodating both the nature of the shooter and the nature of the game.

The qualities we most admire in game birds have much to do with how skillfully they interact with their environments in order to survive. Witness the woodcock's splendid ability to weave in three dimensions through a tangle of alders or the uncanny knack that a cock pheasant has for being somewhere other than where he ought to be. Wariness, strength, and aerobatic expertise all play certain roles in defining which birds are game and which aren't.

Quail seem to hang out in a greater variety of environments

than any of the others. Sometimes you find them, like pheasants, in row-crops and grassland. They also get along fine in the woods, like grouse and woodcock, and in the brush country of the Southwest, which in some ways amounts to a combination of both. Depending upon the cover and the mood they're in, bobwhite can hold as tightly as woodcock or flush as wildly as a herd of March hares.

B UT quail are quail, and once in the air, they behave much the same way, no matter where you find them. Flight, for the most part, is a quail's second line of defense, to be exercised when immobility and camouflage don't work. Bobwhite is a sprinter, not a marathon man, and those broad, stubby wings can take him from a standstill to top speed in short order. The noise they make isn't as loud as a grouse's wings, but it's loud enough, and a whole covey going up at once makes a shocking racket. And there's the visual confusion of all those little, buffy-brown bodies buzzing this way and that. All good, useful tools for survival.

On the other hand, a bobwhite's top speed isn't all that fast compared with some other birds, and even though he can dodge and weave fairly well in the woods, he tends to fly in a straight line toward some piece of escape cover he knows about. Compared with a grouse or a woodcock or a dove, a quail has the maneuvering ability of a tombstone.

Flush some quail without a gun in your hands, and you wonder how you could ever miss one; take a gun along, and some days you wonder why you came. How you react to them is an important factor in how well you shoot quail. Even after all these years, flushing quail startle me, put me momentarily off-balance – especially if I'm anticipating a flush. Then, because they're small and appear to move a lot faster than they really do, some synapse in my skull shifts from torpor to hyper-reactive, and I start handling the gun like a man under attack by a swarm of hornets.

Popular opinion seems to have it that the less weight there is in a gun, the better it is for quail. Not for me it isn't, and maybe not for you, either. One of the reasons why I'm only a middling quail shot is that I shoot too quickly, desperate to connect before the birds reach light-speed and disappear through a hole in the universe. So why do I need an ultralight gun that I can whip around even more aimlessly? I waste enough powder and shot as it is.

I know how big a quail is and how fast it flies, and I can remind myself of all the facts over and over again, but when the birds are in the air, it all goes out the window, likely as not. So, I do my best work on bobwhite with a gun that has some heft to it, one that offers some resistance to jumpy muscles, a gun that forces me to swing instead of inviting me to poke. I can shoot other birds pretty well with a gun that weighs less than six pounds, but not quail. There, a little extra mass is a big help.

Assuming, of course, that it's in the right place. A few years ago, I spent an afternoon shooting quail with a borrowed Winchester Model 50, probably the best-built autoloader that Winchester ever made. Actually, I spent the afternoon shooting *at* quail, for the most part, because the Model 50 also is the most wretchedly balanced gun ever made, at least in my hands. The buttstocks are full of recoil-damping gimmickry; it may well reduce the kick, but it also makes the gun obnoxiously butt-heavy. I felt as if I were holding a barbell in my right hand and nothing at all in my left, so it was equally easy to overpower the muzzle and shoot too far in front or to stop altogether and shoot behind.

The Model 50 (and its weird spawn, the Model 59, the one with the fiberglass barrel) is an exception. Most repeaters suffer just the opposite problem – too much weight out front – thanks to the magazine tubes slung under the barrels and stuffed with springs, plugs, and cartridges-in-waiting. Guns balanced too far toward the nose are slow to get moving, although a little weight forward does help keep the muzzle in motion once you get it started. If you do your quail shooting in open country and if the majority of your shots are fairly long ones, say thirty yards or more, a gun balanced slightly toward the muzzle will noticeably help you track a small target smoothly and swing through for the shot.

Trap guns are built on the same principle for exactly that reason, and there are some useful similarities between quail shooting and trap. A bobwhite and a clay target are roughly the same size and fly much the same way. Which is not to say that the typical trap gun would be anything but a pain in the neck as a quail gun, but the same concepts can apply.

Most quail shooting, though, is more diverse, taking you from open field edges to dense brush, giving you close-in shots and long ones, and you have to deal with angles that you'll never see on a target range. The only way one gun can truly accommodate all that is with a balance that puts equal portions of its weight into both of the shooter's hands.

OUR old buddy and his silvery Model 12 notwithstanding, balance and weight combine as the factor that most mitigates against repeaters as quail guns. No doubt that would come as a great surprise to the uncountable millions of quail that have died at the business end of pump guns and autoloaders and certainly to the only slightly more-countable millions of shooters who've done the work. The point isn't that you *can't* shoot quail with a repeater, but rather that the optimal combination of weight and balance will be a lot easier to achieve with a double.

The only practical way to distribute the weight of a repeater equally between the hands is to add weight to one end of it or the other. Most of them are nose-heavy to begin with, and there really isn't any good way to remove the extra weight. The alternative is to pack enough lead into the buttstock to bring the balance point where you want it – which makes an already-heavy gun heavier yet.

A double, on the other hand, can be built to eliminate every unnecessary ounce of weight and can be balanced to a gnat's whisker. Besides, for sheer liveliness and a handling quality that's almost beyond description, there's nothing like a double. Whether it's a side-by-side or an over-under makes no difference, although over-unders tend to be a bit heavier, gauge for gauge and gun for gun, than side-by-sides. Shoot the one that feels best.

Barrel length can be a factor, depending upon who made the gun. If it's an American piece, chances are you'll want short barrels, simply for a bit less weight. A European gun most likely will be light enough, even if it has thirty-inch tubes. If the weight and balance are right, barrel length isn't important.

Choke isn't really important, either, except that any more than a little is decidedly too much. Most quail are shot inside twenty-five yards, and at that distance skeet and skeet is a great combination. So is cylinder and improved-cylinder. If the local birds often give you longer shots, cylinder and modified will do the trick. The old wheeze about blown patterns from cylinder-bored barrels is utter nonsense; the English have been boring barrels without choke for generations, and there's no better choice for close-range work.

Similarly, the English learned long ago that no one can shoot game at the peak of his ability unless his gun fits. By virtue of the way we shoot them, doves and ducks usually offer a slack moment or two for settling into a stock that doesn't quite fit; pheasant often do, too, because they aren't all that fast on the flush and usually flush in the open besides. But the birds that get out of range or out of sight in a hurry – grouse and woodcock and quail – put a premium on gun fit.

Concentration is one great key to hitting any moving thing with a charge of shot, and quail are the most demanding of all. When a covey comes up, with all its unnerving uproar, you have to check the whereabouts of your companions, know where the dogs are, get your feet in the right position and yourself in balance, pick one bird that offers a safe shot and stay with it, even though there may be another rattling past your nose or flying up your pantleg. With all that going on at once, you don't need the additional handicap of an ill-fitting gun. Keeping your concentration focused is hard enough; if you have to shift your attention from the bird to the gun barrels and back again to the bird, you might as well save a cartridge.

Even if you can't afford to have a quail gun custom-built from scratch, you can have almost any gun altered to a perfect fit. Stocks can be shortened, lengthened, shaved down, built up, and bent to just the right elements of length, drop, pitch, and cast to make the gun point exactly where you look. Stock-fitting is a specialized, demanding skill, and not every gunsmith or even every stockmaker can do it. But there are some good ones around. If shooting is important to you, a session with a good fitter and a try-gun, with the results translated to your own gun, is the best investment you can make.

A gun that fits allows you to concentrate on shooting. A covey rise is complicated business, but there are some ways to simplify things a bit and, if not give yourself an advantage (the bird has most of those, no matter what you do), then at least trim down the number of disadvantages. Pick a bird on the edge of a flushing covey or one that veers off from the rest. If you're not looking into the swarm of feathers and wings, you'll be less distracted by it, better able to keep yourself focused on taking *a* quail – and you have to shoot quail one at a time.

If you kill the first one, then look for another that might be headed in the same direction. Assuming you had your feet properly set up for the first shot, you're already in balance for the next. Quail don't give you much time for foot-shuffling,

especially on a second shot in thick cover.

If you miss the first shot, swing on the same bird for the second. There are two advantages in this. The most common ways to miss a quail are shooting behind it and shooting over it; in the first instance, you stopped the gun; and in the second, you raised your head off the stock. The second shot, if it's at the same bird, is likely to be better because, for one thing, you're already focused on that bird, which by now is escaping at a good clip, and for another, you'll shoot more instinctively. You'll tighten down on the gun, go for the bird with your left hand, and slap the trigger the instant the barrels catch up with it. In short, you'll do what you should have done the first time. The inertia of the quick swing will automatically work out the lead and follow-through, so you'll sweep through the target – and swinging through is the best way to consistently hit bobwhite or anything else, the sustained-lead school of skeet shooting be damned.

If you're shooting over a good pointing dog, you can set up your shot in advance. Quail sometimes do weird things, but a covey in its home range has a set of escape coverts that it normally uses, and the majority of the birds will head toward one of them at a covey flush. Neophyte quail hunters often make the mistake of assuming that the birds will flush in whatever direction the dog is pointing. Not so. They'll flush toward escape cover, whether it's straight away, off to the side, or right up Old Groaner's nose. You won't always know their ultimate destination, because it may be several hundred yards away, but you can often predict the route they'll take from where you find them to where they want to go – into a patch of woods next to a grainfield, toward an evergreen thicket, toward the brushiest part of the woods, across a stream – almost always in the direction that offers the most protection.

So, assuming you're in cover where the birds feel secure enough to sit tightly and assuming that the dog will hold the point, you often can approach from the angle most likely to offer a straightaway shot. If you're hunting with a partner, taking a moment to choose a good approach is especially important; looking things over beforehand helps give you both a chance for reasonable, safe shots. You also can divide up the likely field of fire so you don't end up shooting at the same bird.

Only one of you needs to walk in for the flush. Usually, it's the man who owns the dog, but you can take turns if you want. Most dogs don't care who boots the birds up. Dogs *do* care about the unpleasant surprise of unseen guns blasting in their ears, though, so always take care to approach at an angle where the dog can see you. Circling out and walking straight up in front often helps pin edgy birds and also helps keep the dog steady. But even if they're going to fly straight away, never, ever, walk up a dog's tail and shoot right over his head. It's the sure sign of a beginner and a lovely way to undo a lot of careful training.

WHEN the covey is broken up and you're after a few singles, your shooting probably will improve. Mine does. Single birds aren't nearly as demanding of concentration and don't rattle your equanimity the way coveys do. They, too, are likely to fly toward escape cover, so a good approach can help. Here, you and your partner really should take turns, hit or miss. There's not much sport in two people banging away at one small bird.

Singles give you an opportunity to see exactly how quail behave in the air, how fast, or slowly, they actually fly. You can learn a lot by standing to one side and watching someone else shoot singles, and it should give you a sense of rhythm that will help your own shooting. When a single pops up right underfoot, I find good use in the old English pheasant-shooter's trick of saying to myself, "Oh, what a beautiful fellow you are" as I start the gun moving. It gives the bird a moment to get out where the pattern has some spread to it and gives me the proper cadence for the slow start and quick finish necessary to make the swing-through shooting technique work. I wish I could remember to do it on covey rises.

The gun matters, but probably the worst thing that can happen to any quail shooter is to fall in love with the wrong gun and get into a mind-set that gives the gun itself priority over the purpose it's meant to serve. It happens all the time – or at least it's happened to me often enough.

In much younger days, caught in the whirl of sheer enthusiasm and romance, I wanted more than anything to own a Parker gun, specifically a Parker quail gun. Accumulating the wherewithal took a good while, but that only served to make desire all the keener. By the time I had as much money as I could possibly justify spending on a gun, I'd hopelessly boiled my brain in the Parker mystique. I was convinced that I'd need only take it out of the case and birds would come tumbling from the sky.

The gun was a VHE 16-gauge, factory-built with twenty-six-inch barrels and a single trigger. It had been well-used but well cared-for, and it was a by-God Parker, right down to the dog's head buttplate. I laid four, hundred-dollar bills on the dealer's counter (as I said, this was long ago) and left feeling giddy as a mail-order bride.

There were some problems, as I soon learned. The stock was too short and too low in the comb, and those short, graceful barrels were choked tighter than an owl's backside. And of course there was the image I had – of seeing myself as a wizard with my Parker gun. The biggest problem, though, was that I saw myself being seen being a wizard with my Parker gun, and that was the tolling of doom.

At the time, I subscribed to the silly notion, still popular in some quarters, that altering a factory gun is some manner of cardinal sin. That may be true of minty collector's pieces, but the vast majority of old guns don't qualify. If I had that Parker now, the stock would be bent and lengthened, and the chokes would be little shavings on some barrelsmith's floor. I don't have it, though, and don't care to ever see it again, because instead of insisting that the gun fit me, I resolved to adapt myself to the gun and in the process made myself thoroughly miserable.

The worse I shot, the harder I tried, and naturally, the harder I tried, the more feckless the results. Being, even then, a quick study, it only took three years of sowing aimless lead across the landscape to decide that I'd enjoyed as much of the Parker mystique as I could stand. It wasn't the gun's fault, obviously, but I've never felt quite right about Parkers since. I've suffered through the same nonsense with other guns, but not for long.

Those of us who love fine guns for what they are as well as for what we do with them are always susceptible to that sort

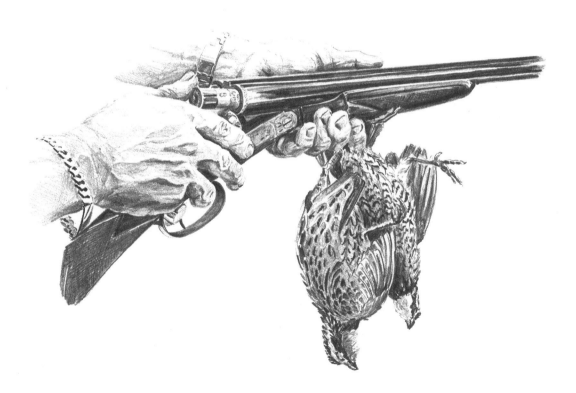

of infatuation, and it's harmless so long as we remember that there's nothing inviolable about a gun. Messing around with a mint-condition American classic isn't a good idea economically, because it's worth more money left as it came from the factory. But if you want a shooter, buy one that isn't mint and have it altered and refinished to your fit and your taste. The same is true of a London Best, except in that case you're justified in having even a mint-conditioned gun altered. London Best guns always have been built for individual customers, not for inventory, and Best guns that change hands in England go back to the maker or to someone else to be fitted to the new owner and probably reconditioned as well. There's no reason why you shouldn't do the same. That's what guns are for.

Guns also are for quail, of course, and that poses a certain dilemma. In lots of places where bobwhite once abounded, quail songs now are sadly faint and few. Central Missouri, where I live, is one of those places, and if I had to depend upon the wild birds I could find within fifty miles of home, I'd be an even worse quail shot than I already am. I'd still keep a dog, but only because I cannot imagine living for more than a week without a sweet Brittany girl to nose my hand in the morning, curl up in my lap at every chance, and snooze behind my chair while I work.

Bobwhite responds beautifully as a cash crop, which is well, because if it weren't for plantation birds, a lot of quail hunters and dogs would find precious little opportunity to hone their skills. Even at that, anyone who wants to stay in shooting trim probably will have to do so with something other than live birds. Some stations on a typical sporting clays course are excellent practice for shooting quail. A trap range is, too, if you can safely walk right up to the house and have the puller release the targets at random. It's not quail shooting, but it's close enough to help refine both your gun and the way you handle it.

QUAIL have been part of my life since the days when I stumped along over the southern-Iowa hills with my father, scarcely taller than his knee-high boots. On the fact of it, the time and energy I've spent fussing with dogs and quail guns would hardly seem to justify the results; only another quail hunter can truly understand why a six-ounce bird is worth all the trouble. Other birds entice me toward adventure. Bobwhite leads me always in a circle back toward home.

I miss the time, not so long ago, when I could walk out the back door or drive a couple of miles down the road and know that I could find a covey or two in an hour's walk. But those days are gone from this patch of country, so October and I spend a lot of time on the road, do as much plantation shooting as we can, and otherwise satisfy our fondness for quail by fooling around with the house covey.

October, who thinks the smell of quail is the most entrancing thing this side of Hi-Pro and cowflops, can't understand why I never hit one of the birds she finds in the rose thicket at the bottom of the pasture or in the cedars on the ridge behind the house. She knows I'm not that bad a quail shot, no matter what I tell her.

CHAPTER FOUR

Quail in the Heartland

by
Tom Huggler

I T SEEMED COMFORTABLY FAMILIAR being a spectator at a high school basketball game after years of playing and coaching the sport myself. We, too, played a racehorse game in a crackerbox gym just like this one in southwest Missouri. Basketball is *supposed* to be played in dinky gyms where the always-combustible fans camp on top of the action and contribute to the game's ebb and flow. There, you can hear the sneakers squeaking; you can smell the honest smell of Lanoline wafting up through bleachers so packed you can hardly see the faces of the cheerleaders doing a stunt.

But I can imagine them as well as picture myself on the playing floor, the ball in my hands, now, with the score tied and the clock ticking down. My desperation rainbow shot at the buzzer has the fans gasping and then moaning "Ooooooooo!" as the ball caroms off the iron and misses.

"Well, it's only the end of the first half," I say to David

Denayer, my host, who is sitting next to me.

"Shoot, yeah," David says. "They'll blow 'em away in the second half. I told you – we got one helluva team this year."

But I wasn't in town just for the game. David also had told me about the fabulous quail hunting in the old strip mines that are tucked away in the rolling back country where he was born forty-some years before. That was back in turkey hunting camp, though, the previous spring, when I had first met him.

"You got to come back this fall and hunt bobwhites," David kept saying. "They quit mining the coal twenty, thirty years ago, and it's all grown back to brush now. In one day, I'll show you more quail than you can shoot at in a week."

I did come back, knocking on the Denayers' door late one Sunday evening while a sleet storm howled around me. David and his wife, Wanda, good prairie folk, took me in and gave me a hot supper and a warm bed, and David made good on his promise to show me out-of-this-world quail gunning the very next day. Although it rained nonstop, David, his brother-in-law Gary Sears, and I tramped for miles, up and over the "dumps" – the name the local people have given to the strip-mined hills and their dangerous pits full of dark water. The footing is treacherous in the dumps, especially when you stumble across wet, black boulders that shine like the coal that was once here in abundance.

Every hour that day, it seemed, the sodden sky would lose another f-stop of light, for this was the day before Thanksgiving, and the winter solstice was approaching.

The strip-mined hills of southwestern Missouri ("Missourah" if you're a native) are edged with fescue grasses and thickets of dogwood, black locust, and grapevines, and on the crowns of the hills grow persimmon and sumac with their ripe, bloody heads, and here and there a cedar. The heavy rains, which had been falling off and on for days, had orphaned fields of standing corn and soybeans. The quail didn't care. They had plenty of wild sunflower, ragweed, native prairie grasses, and lespedeza to eat.

We moved birds all day, although the quail were as reluctant to fly as we were to quit hunting them. Along a hedgeapple row connecting two hills, our five dogs – soaked and steaming in the rain – went on a gang point. Buster turned to stone like some statue, his bobbed Brittany tail quivering. Low-slung Duke, looking like an elastic band stretched to the snapping point, and my own two setters – Macbeth and Chaucer, their respective tails looking like a question mark and an exclamation point minus the dots.

Even Pretty Girl, David Denayer's setter, only four months old, stopped a minute to snoot the scent coming off a huge covey of birds and felt her eyes water for the first time.

There isn't a bird hunter alive who does not love the hair-trigger tension of such moments. You remember thinking, *There is so little time. Not enough time* to get the gun up and follow through in one easy motion. But you do it anyway, in spite of the bulky clothing and the blur of targets that double and triple in your water-streaked shooting glasses. And the birds fall and the dogs turn into vacuum cleaners that make wet, sucking sounds as they nose out the quail and retrieve them to hand.

Those were the limit birds. An hour later, with the dogs toweled down and drying out in the warm kennel, I sit at The Last Straw Cafe in town, dry socks on my feet, stiff fingers cradling a porcelain mug of hot coffee. David says something by way of apology for the turn-down day of crummy weather, but I'm watching raindrops chase one another down the window and smiling that smile that only a happy man who has been to bird hunter's heaven knows.

Such is the grip that hunting bobwhites in the nation's Heartland has been known to get on me, a native of Michigan, which, most observers agree, is a part of an ill-defined region called the American Midwest.

I remember a week-long series of articles I once read on this

subject. Through interviews and observations, the reporters tried to define the boundaries and determine the forces of history, heritage, and culture that make the Midwest what it is. And what is it? Well, they never quite pinned it down exactly. My dictionary is of no help either: *Midwest: n. the Middle West, adj. Middle Western. Also Midwestern.* Equally unenlightening are the synonyms: *America's Breadbasket,* the *Midlands,* the *Heartlands* and *flyover country between the coasts.*

Maybe someone should have asked a bird hunter to define the Midwest. Let me try: "The Heartland has good hunting for pheasants, excellent gunning for forest and plains grouse, and the nation's finest hunting for bobwhite quail." Bobwhite quail? The best hunting? Even better than the South where quail are king?

Yes, in fact *much* better than the South. Consider this: Most people don't know that Oklahoma annually vies with Texas for leadership among the states in bobwhite harvest. Since Oklahoma can be considered part of the Midwest, then the states of Illinois, Iowa, Kansas, Missouri, Nebraska, and Oklahoma bag nearly *twice* as many birds a year as do the traditional states of Georgia, South Carolina, North Carolina, Mississippi, Kentucky, Tennessee, and Alabama.

M OST hunters just don't think of the Heartland when they think of quail. And true, there is no tradition, no hunting heritage of sorts, for gunning bobwhites there. In the South, on the other hand, the bobwhite is called "Bird." There are no compromises and no seconds to Bird. The best hunting is found on manicured plantations, reminiscent of the fine shooting estates in England.

Protocol is likewise observed. A huntmaster directs the action with all the authority and importance of a British headkeeper. Men in white coats may drive the gunners' wagon, which is pulled by mules or slow-stepping horses, while other men in white coats handle the dogs. Only high-born dogs are used – unblooded animals are about as welcome as coonskin caps in church – and a sleek Labrador retriever often handles the fallen birds.

You don't see such scenes in the Midwest; there most quail hunters wear the same Carhatt coveralls they use for doing chores. No tweeds of the northern ruffed grouse woods here. Rather, the men wear faded Levis with permanent Copenhagen rings on the rear pocket. You see few fancy, side-by-side doubles with the kind of delicate engraving skilled craftsmen put on jewelry. Instead, you see "prairie traditional": Poly-chokes hanging on the ends of 870 Wingmaster pumps with scratched stocks and shiny triggers.

Maybe we need a quail-hunting tradition in the Midwest to help save the remaining habitat from chisel plowing and mowing. Get the Fortune 500 companies to buy up the big farms and turn from agribusiness to the business of raising more and better bobwhite hunting. Then again, maybe we should leave it like it is – open to every man with a weekend off and the ability to get a farmer to smile back and swing wide the welcome gate.

On a hunt in Kansas one time, I knocked on the doors of eight farmers who had posted "No Hunting" signs on their land. Seven let me hunt; the eighth was so apologetic at turning me down that I felt sorry for him. In Iowa, an old widow woman invited me in for tea after I gave her a dressed brace of quail and a pheasant as a thank-you for letting me, a complete stranger, walk her bird-infested farm. It was the first wild game she had touched since her husband died years before. In Illinois, my hosts took me to dinner and wouldn't let me pay for my own meal, let alone theirs. In Oklahoma, after we cleaned quail in the back room, the landowner made a barbecued rib run to the nearest restaurant, which happened to be twenty miles away. In Nebraska, a farmer climbed down off his combine and walked over to my car where I was sitting,

watching him work. Noticing my out-of-state license plates, he said, "Howdy. Looking for a place to hunt?"

Precisely at noon, all Heartland farm work ceases for an hour. Each year on the day after Thanksgiving, we hunt on a farm in Webster, Iowa, where the folks put on a noon dinner (it would be sacrilegious to call it a "lunch") that has us staggering through the afternoon hunt. Sure, that kind of down-home hospitality goes on in other parts of America too, but I like to think it is just a common courtesy, a business-as-usual way of doing things in the Midwest.

It is not the bobwhite quail but the gaudy cock pheasant that is the king of Heartland cornfields. Why, I'm not sure, because in many states the number of quail harvested far exceeds the number of pheasants bagged. Maybe it's because pheasants are tougher, cagier, harder to kill. Maybe it's a question of size; Midwesterners are used to seeing things on a grand scale, and they have some of the greatest vistas on the continent, exceeded perhaps only by those in portions of the West. A six-ounce bird can get overlooked, I suppose, when there are two-pound prairie grouse and three-pound pheasants to shoot at.

Then again, population swings make the bobwhite a less-than-stable Heartland resident. Quail are perhaps our most fragile game birds, and Middle America is the northernmost fringe of the bird's range. A decade ago, terrible back-to-back weekend snow and ice storms knocked their number down by ninety-five percent in Ohio, northern Indiana, and southern Michigan. Bobwhites are just now beginning to recover in these areas where they always have had and always will have a tenuous toehold. In other Heartland states where the birds are more plentiful, a breeding stock of just twenty-five percent can bounce back to near capacity in a single year when the birds are blessed with a mild winter and a reasonably warm and dry spring.

Thank God for the bobwhite's resiliency.

Some researchers believe that quail and grouse were likely the same bird several million years ago. They split, the theory goes, along evolutionary lines of climate and habitat. Grouse had their speciation in the northern hemisphere, and that is why their range is circumpolar in the northern temperate zone. Quail, on the other hand, had their speciation in the southern hemisphere. The United States is home to six species. Mexico and Central America have nine more, and there are fifteen other kinds living in South America.

The theory also accounts for the fact that the Midwest, a veritable melting pot with its temperate climate and diversity of habitat, is home to two species of native quail (bobwhites and scaled or blue quail) and three species of native grouse (ruffed grouse, prairie chickens, and sharptails).

Another consideration: In some respects the bobwhite is as much a foreigner to the Midwest as is the pheasant. Bobwhites spread by virtue of colonization. When the Europeans first dropped sounding lines off the North American coast, quail and wild turkeys were two of many strange birds they encountered. The forests that gave way to fire, axe, and plow were quickly replaced by pastures and cropfields, which were criss-crossed in turn by farm lanes and roads. Especially in the Deep South and Middle Atlantic states quail thrived, but they also made their way as far north as southern Michigan, Wisconsin, and Minnesota and as far west as Kansas and Oklahoma. The hunting ethic in the South that began early with the European influence of fine guns, blooded dogs, and landed gentry didn't migrate north and west with the quail.

Why not? Because pioneers didn't have the time or the gunpowder to waste on little birds.

I cannot imagine hunting quail, in the Heartlands or anywhere else for that matter, without a dog. After all, wherever they are found, bobwhites were designed with bird dogs in mind. I like to hunt them later in the year – in January and February (if legal) – when crops are in the elevator and the ground is frozen and the covers have shrunk to manageable size. By then, most of the other hunters have given it up for another year. Statistically, we know that three-fourths of all hunting activity occurs in November and December, even though the quail hunting season is open through January in most places.

LIKE most other game birds, Heartland quail leave the roost shortly after daylight and fly or walk to breakfast. Likely feeding spots include the edges of corn, soybean, wheat, or milo fields, especially those fields that contain weeds or are at least near escape cover of weeds or brush. Other good spots are fields with wild sunflower, ragweed, native prairie grasses, and forbs. The birds eat early and long on days when a storm is brewing. When their crops are full, the quail move to a loafing area such as a field edge or farm lane only a jump away from safe, heavy cover. Here they bask in the sun and preen and delouse themselves for several hours. By midafternoon they are back in the feeding spot where they stuff themselves until nearly dark, then return to the roost.

We start at midmorning, after a leisurely breakfast, and first look for birds in typical feeding areas and then in loafing habitat. Edge covers between crop and weed fields, and weed fields and brushlands are likely places to find them. I never pass up linear connective cover, such as weedy fencerows and hedgerows of osage orange (hedgeapples) and multiflora rose. Thickets and weedy patches along stream bottoms and sloughs where the plow and center-pivot irrigation rigs can't go are other good spots. Early in the morning and late in the day, the roosting areas of grasses and weeds mixed with low bushes (quail like canopy cover from hawks and owls) are productive, too. Care, however, should be taken not to scatter coveyed quail late in the day, especially during bouts of cold weather. Otherwise, the separated birds can easily become winter statistics.

An old practice honored by many quail hunters is never to shoot a covey down below fifty percent. That may not be enough of a safeguard, however. In marginal Midwest habitat where surviving birds are forever forced into shrinking winter security cover, the grim reaper knocks often and hard. Many birds that don't end up temporarily warming the kidneys of successful hunters end up as hawk and owl snacks. Hunting, then, in these marginal areas is not always as compensatory as we would like to think.

Another consideration is that coveys often mix as winter wears on. Shooting them down to fifty percent again and again means you could be eliminating key breeding stock. The only way to avoid that is to know each covey and the number of birds in each before the hunting opener and then monitor the population throughout the season.

I believe that healthy Midwestern quail coveys tend to run larger than elsewhere, but I have no scientific proof to back up my observations. However, I can assure you of this: I don't shoot into coveys containing fewer than ten birds or so. I have further noticed that busted coveys in the Heartland tend to scatter less than those in the South. I don't know if this behavior is because most Midwestern covers are linear, or because quail there are more "herd bound" than elsewhere. Maybe both. I do know that it can be a simple matter to find the pieces of the covey again and again, and have seen pheasant hunters, joyous at finding "bonus quail," shoot them down to numbers that made me nervous.

As for guns and loads, it seems to me the 20 and 28 gauges were designed for quail and quail hunters. I prefer over-under guns that are light (six pounds or so), fast, and well-balanced. Improved cylinder and modified work best overall, but I am not against screwing in choke tubes of skeet and improved cylinder early in the season when flushes are in the face. Later, when the birds get edgy and sometimes run and flush ahead of points, I might opt for modified and modified. I don't

believe you need a full choke barrel for bobwhites.

No. 9 shot in a target load is my first choice in fall. If I can't find 9s, I'll buy No. 8 shot. The dense patterns thrown with either are effective at straining through leaves and brush, but if pheasants are on the hunting menu, I'll grab a pocketful of No. 7½ copper-plated shot in a field load. Copper-plated shot has tremendous penetration; although you don't usually need it for quail, it can be effective late in the year when the birds are heavily feathered and flush at greater distances.

The Heartlands are ripe with good places to hunt quail. The better gunning occurs on private land, but there are fair to excellent opportunities on public land, too, especially late in the season when birds move onto the state-managed properties for food and security.

Each of the Midwestern states that hold quail are subject to the vagaries of weather, the hatch, and game department regulations. But, a few truths come through, year after year.

In Iowa, quail traditionally occur in their greatest numbers in the south, with the south-central region being the best. Consider, too, the downstate two tiers of counties which make up the southern pasture belt. In a good year, Hawkeye State hunters will take a million quail; in a fair to average year, the figure is about half.

Public lands are worth checking out, but don't be afraid to knock on doors, especially later in the season. The season typically opens on the first Saturday in November (along with pheasants) and usually runs through January.

Missouri hunters traditionally take between 1.2 million and 3.9 million bobwhites; the season typically runs from November 1 through mid-January. Best hunting shapes up north of the Missouri River, but the west-central prairie region is also good. The poorest hunting occurs in the southern Ozark region, although public hunting lands containing abandoned fields and bottomlands are worth checking out.

In an average year Kansas quail hunters will bag a million

birds, but the figure can top three million when good conditions make for a bumper crop. The best place to go is in the southeastern region, although good numbers of birds are typically produced in the east-central Flint Hills area and in the northeast, south-central, and southwest.

The season usually opens on the second Saturday in November and runs through January. The western third of the state usually opens later. In the extreme southwestern corner, hunters will find scaled quail in addition to bobwhites. The best place to go is the Cimmaron National Grassland. At 200,000 acres, it makes up about half of the public land in the Sunflower State, 98 percent of which is privately owned, so you'll have to ask permission in Kansas.

In Nebraska, only about one percent of the real estate is public property. Bobwhites are found mostly in the south, although there are huntable numbers across the state. The season usually opens on the first Saturday in November and runs through January. In an average year, gunners will kill a half-million bobwhites. In a good year, they will take more.

As mentioned, Oklahoma hunters may bag more bobwhites than any other state. During a recent survey period, the average hunter shot between seventeen and thirty birds. Besides bobwhites, which are found statewide, the southwestern region and the Panhandle are home to fair to good numbers of scaled quail. The best hunting for bobwhites occurs in the west-central and southeastern areas.

Lease hunting is common because less than three percent of the land base is publicly owned and open to hunting. The season traditionally opens on November 20 and ends in early to mid-February.

Illinois is a real sleeper – often with a kill equal to Iowa and Nebraska combined. The best hunting occurs on private land in southern and western counties. The season opens early to mid-November and lasts until early or mid-January.

There are also quail-hunting seasons in the Heartland states

of Ohio, Michigan, Indiana, and Wisconsin, but bird populations are pretty sparse.

The future for Midwest quail looks good, thanks mostly to the Conservation Reserve Program (CRP), a key part of the 1985 Farm Bill. The CRP provision pays farmers about $45 per acre per year to idle their land for ten to fifteen years, and they are given additional money to plant cover crops to control soil erosion and provide wildlife habitat. More than 25 million acres across the country have been enrolled in the program, which some observers say could do more for game bird production than the Soil Bank program of the 1950s and 60s.

A healthy share of the CRP enrollments are in the nation's Heartlands. Kansas has more than two million acres enrolled, Missouri has 1.3 million acres signed up, and Iowa farmers have committed another 1.6 million acres.

They say Montana is Big Sky Country and, sure, I agree – but so are Nebraska, Kansas, Oklahoma, and parts of Iowa and Missouri. The big vistas of the Midwest nourish big weathers, and over millennia the big weathers and other forces of nature have combined to produce biota that include huge expanses of tall and shortgrass prairie, broken here and there by woody fingers of oak and maple and riparian cottonwood and osage orange. Remnants of the prairies exist, but they have largely been replaced by cropfields and pastures. These areas, too, are as much a home to bobwhite quail as are broom sedge and partridge pea fields of the South.

H OW do you know when you are in the Midwest? Look for chicken-fried steak and blackberry pie on restaurant menus, and keep an eye out for grainfields that seem unending and that are full of crop-eating combines. When cornhusks and wheat chaff litter the highway and when mountains of grain are dumped next to elevators that are already full, you'll know you are there. You'll know, too, when a farmer or rancher (farmers wear seed corn caps; ranchers wear cowboy hats) raises an index finger from the steering wheel in acknowledgment as he passes you in the opposite lane.

Once in the field, you'll know you're there when you see heat waves shimmer on the horizon – and it's only twenty degrees – or when tumbleweeds bounce by and startle you. When you can sense a prairie wind sneaking into your woolen shirt under the hunting jacket, and when you can hear it rattle the papery cornstalks and feel it water your nose and eyes. And you'll know somehow this all seems clean and good and right.

Hunting Heartland bobwhites is an ongoing awareness of what is small and important and what is big and important. Whenever I go there, this happens to me. One minute I'm admiring the way another hunter's dog handles in a coppery field of little bluestem a half-mile away. The next minute I'm separating lespedeza seeds and wondering about the stored-up, quail-growing energy in each. In the distance, on a morning when the air is still as a cemetery, you hear a freight train pounding a loose tie and wonder where that train has been and where it is going. Later, the guy filling your truck at the Sinclair station (Remember the green dinosaur?) tells you about a farmer neighbor of his that might just let a man go hunting, and later still the farmer says, "Heck, yes, you can hunt, so long as you don't shoot into the home covey behind the milking barn."

So there are priorities here, as elsewhere, and somehow a little weight in the game bag from a bobwhite or two makes it all seem normal and most satisfactory. In the end, of course, it all comes down to the people. And the dogs and the guns. And motels where a man can sneak a setter into his room without too much fear of being asked to leave. And restaurant pie, certainly, and high school basketball games.

Speaking of which...we weave our way back to the bleacher seat in that little town in southwestern Missouri just in time for the second-half tipoff. I notice my coat lies exactly where I

left it, and the car keys and sunglasses are still in the unzipped pocket, along with my new driving gloves. As David Denayer had predicted, the game is a blowout in the second half, and the home team wins. They didn't need my off-the-bench, last-second heroics after all.

On our way out the door, we buy a few more homemade cookies from the local athletic boosters, because a man never knows when he'll get hungry in the field tomorrow and David is already talking about how the changing weather is going to make for a better hunting day.

CHAPTER FIVE

Texas Quail: A Fitful Passion

by
David Simpson

HUNTING QUAIL in a dry country is clearly a crapshoot. Down below San Antonio in the brushy ranges of the Rio Grande plain, the little sand chickens are born to die. The main problem is rain, or lack of it. Parts of the *brasada*, the brush country, are probably the best natural bobwhite country in the world when it rains in the spring and again in the fall. When it doesn't, the seed-bearing weeds shrivel and change to dust, and the fat, rich grasses turn brown and curl into hard wire and disappear as the soil shows raw and naked under a resolute sun.

This country toys with the ardent quail hunter who, squinting at the sky like some grizzled sharecropper, eyes the gravid clouds of summer and feels the sultry promise of morning humidity and wonders if it will ever rain again.

And in some years enough rain will come, and it will fall in the right months and the mesquite prairies will have their moments of glory, smelling of flowers and fecundity, the pleached skeletons of brush covered temporarily by verdant growth. Then the cotton rats and the cottontail rabbits appear as if by spontaneous generation, their eyes glowing green at dusk as your headlights sweep the edges of *senderos*. Quail seem to seethe under every bush and lustily buzz out from your car as you drive the narrow dirt roads.

Even in the good years, quail live a perilous existence. They disappear down the gullets of coyotes and bobcats and skunks, or the occasional harrier or great horned owl, and their eggs are crushed by hungry raccoons and are stepped on by the ubiquitous crossbred beef cattle of the country. Chicks, usually as sprightly and precocious as tiny goblins, are sometimes trapped in drying cracks in the heavier soils. Even adult quail can drown during the wild flooding of thunderstorms, or once they are wet, die quickly when it then turns cold. Dry cold agrees with them for a while, but without winter rain, there are no forbs, green plants, to carry them through until spring.

Weakened by lack of food, quail are beset by ticks and mites, roundworms and tapeworms and some thirty kinds of bacterial, viral, mycotic, and protozoan disease. The quasi-mythical population of one bird per acre may be attained in certain areas for short periods of time in the most prime habitat, but one quail per five or more acres is a lot more common. Although it is hard to say how often this bounty might occur, two years in twenty might be a good guess. In the other years there are fairly consistent populations in a few spots, generally nearer the Gulf of Mexico in sandy soils, and wild swings in the other parts of the brush country. There are usually enough birds to hunt, at least before Christmas, but some years will oblige the weaker sport to spend his hunting afternoons drinking gin fizzes at the Cadillac Bar in Nuevo Laredo.

We just finished one of the big seasons, the best I can

N. Booth

remember. I have to laugh at all of my deer hunting friends who suddenly took notice of the birds as if they had seen the Second Coming. They bought new guns and snake boots and vacant-headed pointers and headed for the brush. I find it more practical to turn to other sport than to gnash my teeth at the vagaries of rainfall. Bonefishing, for example, is related to quail shooting in its intensity of the moment: before the take, and before the covey rise. Unfortunately, bonefishing is also a capricious pursuit. You may not catch a bonefish either, but at least you will have had a tropical vacation and won't have to stare at the gaunt, gray bones of a starving country. Some years when there is money and time, I shoot quail in Arizona or Mexico. Take your own pick of ways to get by, but remember that hunting quail here in the cowboy's birthplace is a fitful sort of passion.

•   •   •

WE got an inkling of the big year to come while dove hunting. The previous quail crop had been excellent, and my Labrador Pete had begun to show a geriatric talent for pointing coveys of birds. We had spring rains again, and already the rumors of hordes of bobwhites were beginning to drift up from the Nueces country. I was primed to shamelessly repeat the previous season's pattern of shooting two or three days a week. Divorce and a general period of shiftlessness had pointed out to me the relative importance of afternoons spent away from the office.

My sidekick Anne and I made a date to go shopping on the border, with a swing by our secret dove place on the way back. In the fall, nothing seems as important as wingshooting, and all other activities are bent to allow the opportunity. We did our business and made the standard run by the Cadillac for *cabrito al pastor*. In the middle of the late lunch, Anne threw down her fork and said, "I want to shoot some birds!" This was a woman who was ranching near Blanco and was known to drive sixty miles for enchiladas in an impetuous Mexican food fit. Powerless to resist any sort of compelling case for movement, I left half my goat on the plate and called for the check. We paid off the parking lot attendant in the white glare at the rear of the Cadillac, bought a bottle on *anejo* rum, and beat it across the *puente dos* to the Texas side.

Bobwhite quail are not unlike humans in that they like to gather at hotspots with their brethren. We were to shoot doves that afternoon at such a location, a sort of Club Med of game birds. The place was like this: an intersection of the common corners of three fields, a dirt road, and a railroad track. The track is little used, and the sides of the roadbed are overgrown with luxuriant grass and weeds. The fencerows are choked with prickly pear and sunflower and mesquite. The fields themselves have been invaded by croton, an indicator of disturbed soil, the mature seeds of which a dove will fly twenty miles to eat, if the quail don't get them first. Within one-hundred yards of the corner lay every kind of accommodation a quail could want, including feeding, loafing, and nesting cover and hideouts as thick and forbidding as a stiff wire brush.

We could hear quail calling as we got out to put the guns together. It was hot and as I dumped shells into my game bag, we were surrounded by the burning smell of grass against the catalytic converter. Doves crossed the colorless sky above us with their swift, intermittent flight. We climbed the gravel edges of the track and went down into the dry, deep grass on the other side. A huge covey of bobwhites ejected from underneath our feet and shot into the heavy cover along the fences. We were being tested again by the bulliest, best-fed, and most habituated quail I had met in my career. You could always kill a few young dumb ones from this unruly gang, but the survivors rapidly regained their old habits – roaring off as you closed the truck door, or sucking you into hapless pursuit down the railroad right-of-way, merging into other coveys and

doubling back to call mockingly from the corner.

Quail season didn't open for more than a month and all we could do was wonder at the power of this horde, now swollen by ideal conditions to some thirty birds. We killed our doves and laid them out ceremoniously on the tailgate. The sun became a white hole in the western sky and we stood in the hot, slanting light and plucked the small gray pigeons in great puffs of feathers. I was thinking ahead to the rest of the fall. Things seemed to be lining up just fine.

•   •   •

THE classic form of wingshooting involves a complex of game, country, weather, men, dogs, and guns. Tamper with the formula too much and you get something else. If accused of extremism, with dignity I'll say that I hew to a certain stern code. Killing quail is more than mere divertissement. the recipe, to my own mind, is not inflexible. Add women to the mix and if they like to shoot, okay. But then if your clothes or car become a major component of the complex, it is possibly time to stop and check for a drift into dilettantism.

A form of gun sickness is also permissible, the gun being the extension of ourselves that kills the little birds. You are allowed (encouraged?) to spend untold amounts of money on a gun as long as you will use it. Forget putting your prize on the rack only to watch it gleam dully in the nostalgic light of the gun room. When you stray too far from the act of killing, and eating, game birds and the profound mystery of their deaths, you have left the fold.

In south Texas, the quail shooter of stature, or of passion, hunts with dogs, while the great unwashed stay close to their immense vehicles, sometimes equipped with great conning towers and all manner of external seats and appendages. It's now fashionable to bait ranch roads with corn or milo maize and to shoot into coveys of quail on the ground from such a vehicle. This is a cheap trick and the shibboleths of purism be damned, I wouldn't give ten cents to do it. It is rather efficient, at least until the birds learn to vamoose when they hear a truck coming. Now notice that the vehicle is not part of the classic complex, which after all, is a troublesome way to put a few birds on the table. Are you beginning to get the idea that the most approved and meaningful way to hunt quail is the most expensive, the most burdensome system imaginable?

Dogs are absolutely essential to the classic quail shoot, the trouble they cause mostly being considered a piddling irritation. Personally, I never could love a pointer. The modern English pointer is a marvelous creature of a specified, if rather narrow, talent. Put them on the ground and they will cover the country, sometimes within sight. If you have spent hundreds of dollars to send them to college, they may even stop when they scent birds. Pointers know no off-season. In the neighborhood, they will hunt just like in the field, and killing pet pussycats seems to them a plausible substitute for pointing quail. Pointers are democratic canines and will ignore the most commanding overture played on the Acme Thunderer; the caller is treated with equal disdain, no matter his station in life. As I write this, I am looking out at the dog pens at a dog that last summer flippantly chewed up *hundreds* of dollars worth of fly-tying materials taken from my bench. I could go on.

I didn't hunt quail when I was a child. Our wingshooting target was doves, and anyway, I was raised in a tradition of pursuing bigger game. About the time I was in high school, my father went through some kind of sea change and bought a pointer bitch out of Riggins' White Knight, and we started to chase quail. I despised it. There was all the walking and constant whistling for the dog, and the recoil gave me a headache.

Then the bitch, Kate, had a litter of pups including a prodigy

H. Booth

named Bulldog that could trail a wounded bird across a long stretch of sand and burrs and dig it out of a hole and bring it back. I began to see some sense in this. I went to work as a trap boy at the local gun club and shot up all my earnings on the way to becoming a little shotgun tough and incipient gun snob. After that I decided that I liked shooting things in the air, but that a clay pigeon was a long ways shy of a live bird.

Later, I bought a Labrador retriever, thinking that I would somehow avoid the insulting behavior of pointers, and began to develop my own style of hunting quail. It wasn't in the starched khaki and white tablecloth style that one would be offered at the King Ranch, but it had meaning and we brought home birds. Mostly it involved a lot of walking, but I had begun to like that, too. Pete would hunt close and quarter, but I would read the cover, directing him to investigate any likely spot. After a few seasons of this, as long as he was within sight and voice, we could ease up to a birdy-looking thicket and Pete would wiggle his rigidly held tail and cock his ears if there were birds inside. It was a system that worked well in open country with scattered cover.

One Sunday afternoon a couple of seasons ago, Pete and I stayed at the deer lease after everyone else left. Things were not good at home. I was living alone for the first time in ten years and had no intention of going to the house and sitting in the pallid light of the television when there were quail to be had.

Other than ground-sluicing a few birds for the pot, the hardbitten deer and pig hunters in our group had little interest in the bobwhites, so I had worked out my own patterns for tricking birds. One of the sure ways to temporarily improve quail habitat is to clear mature brush by root plowing or chaining and allow new growth to come in, providing better food and cover for the birds. There were two fields nearby that were in this state, with the addition of tall, improved grasses for nesting cover. We had made a pass or two at them with the pointers, only to have the birds flush wild and hook it uphill into a fortress of thorny *guajillo*. I thought I could do better by walking rather than driving, and I would keep Pete in close and quiet.

After lunch I took a long nap and read in the house trailer while Pete snoozed on the couch. It was a cold day and I felt secure in the bed and didn't want to leave. Getting up from the bunk, I put on jeans and a basket-stamped belt, tucked the pants into my Russell snake boots, slid a wool shirt over long johns, followed by a soft, old ducking jacket and a big silk cowboy wild rag. We still think of this as the West, so a big felt hat went on top.

Outside everything was covered with a strange glaucous light; it was already hard to see. Big leafless mesquites stood along the road, dark and spidery against a low sky. In front of us the overgrown field, a tilted ochre space, lay below the black *guajillo* ridge.

Crossing through a set of cattle pens and a fence, we began to work the field from the ridge side to block the birds from flying into the thicket. About seventy-five yards in, we jumped two birds out of range that fluttered downfield. Pete began to act anxious and birdy and stopped to listen near a stem of running mesquite. Three birds slanted out ahead of him, straining for the ridge, and I killed a pair. I broke the gun and reloaded as Pete retrieved the birds from the heavy, brittle grass. The first was a cock that lay in my hand with a drop of bright blood at the tip of its bill. I thought, "At least I've got a meal."

Working the cover methodically, we made a sweep without incident. We turned to the north fence and came back parallel to the first run. On the third pass, Pete stopped abruptly at a thick place in the grass and went stiff with an intense expression of curiosity on his face. Whoaing him softly, I came up on his right and as I reached him, four birds jumped out about a foot from his nose. They pulled straight away and

again I killed one with each barrel. "Stay," I said, and ejected the empties on the ground behind me. As I closed the gun, another bird, a cock with a distinct white eye stripe and throat patch, rose straight up and as he towered I shot him with a big pop of feathers. The order of things was beginning to approach the miraculous.

Pete had still not moved but was looking fervently at the spot where the last bird had fallen. I ejected the empty, clicked in a shell and saying, "Heel," took a couple of steps. It seemed much darker now, and I was worried about finding all my birds. Then two hens bolted from our left and sped in a shallow crossing trajectory to the right. With three on the ground, I had no business shooting, but reacted anyway and divining more than seeing them, shot one, swung back and then tracked the other for the double. It almost never happens this way and I was prepared for anything to occur next, including the opening of the heavens and a bolt of lightning snaking down through the cowboy crease of my Resistol.

I marked the five birds as best I could and sent Pete, who found the first pair and the single cock. Happy to be working, he returned each bird jauntily. I marked the last pair again carefully and dropped my hat on the ground as a reference and took Pete to the general area. He hunted randomly for several minutes and came back with a hen that was hard hit but still alive. To keep the bird intact, I issued the *coup de gras* by sharply rapping its head on the rubber butt of my gun. My dog was now looking at me with what I took to be a recalcitrant belief that his work was done. I looked back toward my hat and with a fresh bearing, stepped to the last bird, which lay belly down with wings softly spread, its mottled back almost invisible against the weathered grass. As I went to get my hat and empties, I rehashed the shots in abject wonder.

It was past good shooting light by then, and we edged through the taut fence and ambled down the road toward camp. I could feel the weight of the birds in my belt pouch and reached back and touched their feathery warmth just to see if it had all really happened. As we came into the yard, coyotes were whooping it up somewhere in the south end of the pasture, their eerie ventriloquism causing the ruff to stand on Pete's back. I ran the faucet into a bucket for him, turned on the yellow yard light, and then laid the quail out in a row on the picnic table. I sat down and looked at the birds' subdued and elegant plumage and hoped I'd never have to do without this.

• • •

As a measure of the personal meaning of game, I've gotten damn particular whose belly it goes into. *Meat to meat* as the Beduoins say, vegetarians and their ilk taunted and made to feel unwelcome here. During a big season there is always the superabundance of cleaned birds in the freezer, and standards are challenged in the interest of none going to waste. Usually it is only a few carefully chosen practitioners of the blood sports who get the chance when I cook. Those who won't appreciate the difference are likely to get chicken, if that.

My observation is that quail are cooked about as sloppily as they are shot. The favorite regional treatment is to insert a canned jalapeño chili in the body cavity and wrap the entire bird in bacon secured by a toothpick. It's a sufficiently good method that most often comes unraveled when cooked over chemically formed and lit charcoal briquets. The final result is a hydrocarbon atrocity I don't plan to sully myself with again. Here in mesquite and live oak country, wood is so cheap and plentiful that it's only in emergencies that I even use pure mesquite charcoal, lit with kindling or an electric starter.

I've been through the gamut with quail recipes from demi-glaces to casseroles and light game soups to boneless *supremes* with a green pepper sauce. A regional favorite seems to be called for here, something with the essence of the brush

country. Traditionally, I'm not sure that there is such a thing as a refined dish, most camp and ranch food being pretty simple. Down on the border when you order quail to go with a soothing bottle of *Negro Modelo*, it will usually be fried, sometimes grilled.

I don't know its historical antecedents, but the following recipe from Beinhorn's *Mesquite Cookery* reeks of the border country, *la Frontera*, of Texas and Mexico. Basically you marinate the quail, butterflied, in a mixture of good safflower oil, lime juice, and tequila. Before letting them stand a couple of hours at cool room temperature, you complete the marinade by rubbing the birds with crushed chili petines and sprinkle them with bruised fresh thyme. Grill over a mesquite fire that has burned down to red-hot coals for about five minutes to a side. As with most game, don't overcook.

•   •   •

AND what of the big season? It has quickly turned apocryphal in my memory and seems as distant as a childhood dream; yet there is a clarity and seamlessness about the whole thing. It was going to the office in snake boots on Tuesdays and Thursdays and sneaking out by 2 o'clock. It was coming home in the dark with a wan sliver of tired moon hanging over the western hills. It was driving all the way to Hebbronville in Anne's 460 Ford pickup, eating embueltos at Frank's place, and stumbling out at six a.m. to shoot quail over white dogs that ran like ghosts in the early fog. It was a thirsty Pete on a hot day, standing and trying to scent a dead bird that lay between his feet. Kenny Krueger ran a string of thirty-two birds for thirty-seven shots and one day I killed fourteen for seventeen. It was working the big field with the boys at the deer lease and having the huge coveys trading back and forth like clouds of blackbirds. Quail frozen in blocks of ice began to crowd out the venison in the freezer. Finally, Kenny and I ended it all in the desiccation and ninety-degree heat of the last day of February, chasing coveys of birds we had not even seen all season.

• • •

That was a year ago and things in Texas have changed. It didn't rain that winter, and the spring rains were spotty. The country grew bare and hard, and starvation and disease killed the quail. Anne got married and Pete died the day after a dove hunt. We didn't even try to shoot on any of our leases, and most of us stayed closer to the office. Making money seemed to be more important.

Any sadness on my part has been momentary. I had one invitation to shoot in a pocket of country that got rain, and for an afternoon we lived as intensely as before. There is still a chance for rain, and I have a new double gun and a puppy coming. I'm just keeping my passion for Texas quail hunting in check until it is time to let it run free through the *brasada* again.

CHAPTER SIX

Plantations:
The Living Tradition

by
Charles F. Waterman

I T IS DIFFICULT to hide a yacht, but a Big House can be a long way up a sand road. Quail plantation folks do it without much advertising, and a Big House can be almost camouflaged in the piney woods, along with the stables and kennels. On the other hand, there are plantation owners who say to heck with it and go ahead with the white columns and the landscaping, even if they do stay off the highway.

Plantation owners often have no title other than Board Chairman, but sometimes there are neckties along with occasional tweeds, weather permitting. I can't help comparing this plantation business to British gunning, which is regularly cited as the aristocracy of bird shooting. They're so different that a rating is impossible, but in one of my ventures into plantation life I sat beside a Britisher with the driven-partridge background. He loved the dogs and the horses but I felt something was bothering him. He could tell I was an outsider (maybe it was my boots) and when no one else was listening, he spoke up.

The matched mules, guided by a driver in a white jacket, were following a purposely faint trail unobtrusively cleared of brush, and two English pointers were slicing through the woods ahead of handlers on horseback.

"I say," inquired the Englishman, "Isn't there some way we can drive these quail to the gun?"

I stopped short of saying it would be impossible, but it sure wouldn't be easy. I have since wondered how many beaters it would take to keep a few coveys of bobwhites on a predictable course across milo fields, piney woods, and broom sedge patches. And although I'm sure most of the plantation owners and operators have engaged in European shooting from time to time, they have been a little reluctant to change their overall hunting operation much in the last hundred years or so, despite their private jets at nearby airports.

I don't know of any ruffed grouse plantations, despite the ruff's claim to aristocracy, and birds such as the chukar (a European game bird celebrity) are seldom sought with hunt managers, flushing whips, and wagons with hydraulic brakes. Of course, the explanation is that the bobwhite quail adapts uniquely to land management and high-powered pointing dogs while remaining a wild bird. There aren't many pen-raised quail on private plantations. It would make a better story to say there are none at all, but most plantations have a little try at that in special cases, the owners tending to apologize abjectly when slow-goers show up during a hunt.

The Southern quail plantation is a tradition, although not all of them follow the conventional pattern, and there are a lot of quail shooters who don't even know they are still around. I am estimating there are about fifty that follow the traditional style, but there are some that don't have the matched mules and the wagon, turning to four-wheel-drive trucks of various styles. Go far enough south in Florida, for example, and the plantation becomes a "ranch" set in cow country instead of cotton country; slide over into Texas and the operation is huge but hardly traditional and the hats are bigger. For the most part, Scarlett O'Hara would not feel at home there.

Now we who plod on foot through the puckerbrush with the family dog might have a tendency to smirk a little at the plantation folks, what with their entertaining American Presidents and foreign nobility, but they aren't necessarily full-time plantation residents. One of them spends some weeks each year prowling about bird country with a weathered pickup truck, one dog, and a friend, with no neckties and hardly anything made of tweed. Although national political campaigns and corporate mergers may be instigated at plantation headquarters, these people have the same shotgun hankering as the guy who slips through the palmettos after work. And after riding a Tennessee walking horse or a rubber-tired wagon all day, some of these folks will arise in a pre-dawn rainstorm and plunge into a knee-deep swamp after wood ducks.

N OW a quail plantation is just that, often thousands of acres run for the welfare of bobwhites, the dogs that point them, and the people who shoot at them. It ruins some of the gee-whiz elements of my story but it must be confessed there are some parts of some plantations that are devoted to raising things for the market, and the complexities of taxation are too much for me to consider. I suspect the modern private quail plantation came about rather gradually, quail being a happy by-product of big farming and the gentry who controlled it. But that's only logical guessing and proof would involve delving into land records of more than a hundred years ago.

I suppose some wealthy planters got farther and farther away from the home place, and while they were involved in things other than cotton, peanuts, tobacco, or cattle they just didn't want to give up traditional quail shooting. This is only guessing, and uninformed guessing at that. Anyway, there

came the plantation to be run for the bobwhite alone, and it may be that when quail are no longer available to the brushpatcher or the swamp buggy, Gentleman Bob will continue to thrive on his own land, managed by students of his welfare. Think on that.

The commercial plantation is a different program, of course, despite appearances, but one operator said he didn't build his for profit but to save some quail hunting for the public. I'm quite sure the wolf had not approached his door.

I guess I hadn't really thought about traditional plantations quietly going about their business until someone invited me to a field trial many years ago and gave me directions that led away from the main roads, but not really very far from supermarkets and condominiums.

"This is for shooting dogs, and the plantation managers have some of these trials every year after the season closes," my host said. "The dogs come from the plantations and sometimes some owners show up too."

The house and barn were pretty big and the kennels were large and noisy. There were horses all over the place and there were mules and the wagons I'd never actually seen before. There were some people in cowboy hats and I think it was the first time I'd seen "plantation clipped" horses. The plantation clip keeps horses looking neat in winter without removing the long hair from their lower bodies and running gears, which will come in contact with brush and palmettos. There were English saddles with appropriate boots and riding breeches and quite a lot of tweed. I checked my snake boots and brush pants and said no thanks, that I didn't want to ride a brace and that I'd sit on one of the wagons. "Riding a brace," of course, is field trial talk; it was a field trial, all right, and almost as formal as the big open ones. I might have "ridden a brace," but my horsemanship was a little creaky and I wasn't sure of the etiquette involved in following "shooting dogs."

A "shooting dog" is so close to the wind-burning open-field

trial type that many of his friends and relatives are in the other business. Fact is, many of the shooting dogs run in the big trials when quail season is closed. On that day in north Florida, I watched (at long range) while various pointers and setters made exactly one hundred finds. A hundred-and-one finds would make me sound more truthful, but they just didn't cut it. To this day I don't know if they were all wild birds or partly pen quail. Many years later, I watched plantation dogs find forty-nine coveys in two half-days of shooting, and there were no pens in their background. What we have here is a rare thing – truly intensive game management – and the bobwhite responds to it in a way that wouldn't work with most game birds.

Thomasville in south Georgia is known as a center of quail plantations but they are in much of the South, often surrounded by producing farms of various sizes, and some residents of the immediate areas are likely to be employed on them. When neighbors are shooters they may be delighted with a plantation because the intensive quail management produces an overflow population, making for good neighbors all around. Except for the popping of shotguns, usually in the distance, there's not much about a plantation to disturb the folks next door, but I heard of one plantation owner who got his snake boot in his mouth.

"I just didn't think," he said.

The plantation owner and a guest were going to a nearby town that day on business and there was no time for a full-scale hunt with horses. The staff wasn't prepared for it anyway, but the plantation owner didn't want to waste any hunting time and he knew where there were a couple of coveys on the way to town, so he put a brace of pointers in the car and told his friend expansively:

"These birds are right near the road and this farmer is a friend of mine. We'll just stop off for an hour on the way, get a few birds, and not lose a whole day's shooting."

The neighboring farmer met them with smiles and said of course they could shoot his quail.

"What are neighbors for if you can't do a little shooting on their places?" he said. "I know you feel the same way, and I know that any time my friends and I want to hunt your place you'd make room for us."

The plantation owner checked his watch, said it was getting late and there wouldn't be time for his neighbor's birds that day, but he certainly appreciated the hospitality. I never learned if his neighbor was really interested in working a few thousand acres of professionally managed quail cover or not.

NOW plantation managers tend to be masters of dog handling, students of horseflesh, professionals in employee relations, and diplomats of a high order. They may perform as hunt managers too, sometimes a task of great complexity.

There have been all sorts of horsedrawn "dog buggies," but the traditional plantation wagon is generally pulled by two mules, has the driver up front, and upholstered seats for the shooters just behind him. There are rubber tires and probably hydraulic brakes. Behind the gunners are the compartments for the dogs, arranged so it isn't too difficult to load and unload them in braces or as individuals. Boxes are screened for good ventilation, and some of them have roll-down canvas curtains for bad weather. Handlers generally pick up the dogs by their loose skins, a procedure that might horrify owners of some family pets, but the plantation stock seems to expect it and I have never heard a yip of discomfort there. It's evidently most practical for both dog and man. However, an adult canine who has never encountered such treatment is likely to consider it an indignity and become vocal about it.

The plantation "shooting dog" is probably an English setter or English pointer and most of them would be hard to hunt with on foot. By far the majority are pointers and they are

seldom expected to run for long periods of time, so they don't tend to hold back much. There are cold days, of course, but we're pretty far south and it's more likely to be quite warm. Hard-driving dogs require special attention on hot days and shouldn't be on the ground too long. Handlers are expected to be expert observers and they train as well as handle.

These dogs are not expected to retrieve. In fact, they're often picked up when hunting dead and forcibly sent on their way for another covey. The retrieving is left up to specialists. Sometimes the retriever or retrievers ride atop the dog boxes or seat, and sometimes they have their own compartments, to be released after the shooting. Labradors and goldens are popular for that job, but springer spaniels are used, too. Occasionally, there are Brittany spaniels for the retrieving although generally they're not big-going enough for the pointing tasks. Occasionally, Brittanies point cripples until told to retrieve, but that's not really standard.

These pointing dogs have active careers and despite top-notch handling, living quarters, food, and medical attention, they aren't long-lived. A plantation owner who has had hundreds of them, with a smattering of field-trial champions, says he figures a seven-year old dog is about at the end of its string. Perhaps this is as much a matter of breeding for hard-driving performance as it is a result of plantation life. We'll leave the analysis to veterinarians. The plantations look for the best, and dog-buying is an important part of the manager's job with the owner on top of it in many cases. Despite the Englishman's inquiries about driving quail, bird dogs are the hingepin of the whole operation. I was staring big-eyed about the plantation grounds when a truck full of setters and pointers came up the drive.

"Dog broker," the manager said.

The manager and a shotgun followed the truck in a jeep and they disappeared through some pines. There was considerable gunfire back there that lasted for an hour and then the vehicles returned. Two of the pointers were led toward the plantation kennels. They had tested several of the dogs with released quail and a skilled gunner. Someone wrote a check and the broker drove away – to another plantation, I supposed. It happens the plantation in question was semi-commercial, used as a retreat for its owner and friends, and open to paying guests at other times. Call it a preserve if you want to, but the operation was close to tradition.

It was a veteran plantation manager who offered a sage observation about bird dogs.

"If you run a lot of dogs the way we do here," he said, "the price of good ones is pretty standard. You can go out and pay cash for high-grade winners, you can raise and train pups yourself, or you can buy all kinds of inexpensive dogs and cull them until you get good ones. Over the long haul the price comes out about the same in the end."

It is a sage piece of advice coming from a man in a rather unique position having to produce smooth performers through the years, and needing several of them at a time. Not all plantation dogs are champions and some may not even be registered, but it all comes down to finding the quail the manager knows are there and handling them smoothly.

I am a little short on plantations myself but since I write about bird dogs and shotguns, I have had an opportunity to visit several and may be competent to relate just how a plantation hunt works.

In a full-scale operation there is an outrider for each dog being run and a manager to oversee the whole works in cooperation with the host, who is likely to be on a wagon or a horse. Generally, the hunt manager is mounted. When there is a rider following each dog, mounted guests stay out of the way and back near the wagon.

Following a hard-going shooting dog involves a little steeplechasing since the pace is not always sedate. It's common for horses to fall, and your veteran plantation rider is

114

likely to roll away from trouble in the best rodeo style. Guests sometimes ride Tennessee walkers all right, but efficiency generally supersedes style in horses. Most of them are pretty, all right, but not all have illustrious parentage. They have to put up with gunfire, brush, sometimes soft going, and with riders who may not be in the best form.

Saddles for gunners and staff are generally a sort of modified English style, although some dog handlers prefer the Western stock saddle. When there's to be shooting, somebody holds the horses in most cases, although most of them are trained to stand ground-hitched alone in an emergency. A horseback quail hunter long ago told me that I hadn't "shot" until I had done it that way. I never liked him much.

THE approach of a full-scale plantation hunt is not exactly stealthy. Since they can't keep their dogs in sight at all times, the handlers frequently sing to them. The wagon creaks, the horses blow, and there's considerable conversation. I suppose some canny bobwhites shove off when they hear the hunt coming but it's actually a pretty efficient approach.

It's usual for a handler to call out "Point!" when he has one and some of them have a sense of the dramatic, the signal strong enough to indicate tigers or leopards. One hunt manager wears a big hat and lifts it straight in the air when dogs are on point, a local tradition beloved by the guests. Maybe it's a common gesture, but I've missed it elsewhere.

Points are routinely approached by two shooters. The host or the hunt manager announces who they are, and in the most traditional setup somebody actually hands a shooter his gun if he's in the wagon. The saddle scabbards are a mite hard on fine blueing since the South is full of sand and leather attracts it. The hunt manager tells the gunners where to walk and then approaches the pointed birds with a flushing whip which he may or may not need to use. Sometimes he says, "Mark!" and calls the shooter's name, an unnecessary announcement when a big covey erupts with a sound like ripping cloth. There is no more perfectly organized bird shooting in the world, and I have done the worst shooting of my life on plantations. To me, each flush is an emergency.

There are all sorts of stories of first-timers and their nervousness on plantation shoots. There is the man with the flushing whip who is going to put up your birds and the man holding the horses behind you. There is the shooting wagon and its mules, and the expectant passengers. There is the other shooter. Although all of this is arranged so that the birds should fly in a pre-determined direction, there is the horror of making an unsafe move. Horses or mules blowing give a fine imitation of flushing quail, and there is the old horror story of the poor soul who scored a double on mules – but for the most part the shooting is conducted in a very safe manner. Most of the shooters know how a gun works.

On many hunts there is no effort at all to work singles for a second flush, but that's up to the hunt manager who knows just how much pressure there has been in a given area and has no desire to wipe out a covey.

The traditional gun for plantation shooting is the side-by-side twenty, and the most common load where I've watched is an ounce of number eights. Just as I was about to announce that even an over-under is a plantation crudity, I visited one where the gunrack was a picket fence of twenty-gauge autoloaders. The owner said he liked them. He was a native-born Southerner and explained that the true traditionalists tend to be Northerners. One bobwhite expert, stronger on biology than ballistics, announced it was unsportsmanlike to use anything larger or smaller than a twenty-gauge. The pundit's reasoning was that anything larger than a twenty was overgunning and abusing the game, and that anything smaller was exhibitionism and likely to result in cripples. Although many twelve-gauges are loaded down with an ounce of shot while a twenty can be stuffed with an ounce and a quarter, the small

hole in the barrel is sometimes equated with sportsmanship. I doubt that anyone need blush if, for example, he has nothing but an ultra-light British twelve to bring along.

There is deer hunting and turkey hunting on many plantations and flooded cornfields concentrate ducks. The dove shoots are a full-fledged part of plantation life, and some of the specially planted dove fields have blinds good enough to camp in. There is the startling sight of attendants in red jackets riding into the surrounding countryside to get doves moving, and white tablecloths under the oaks for lunchtime. I have been a little shaken to find my dove blind overseen by a handler with a Labrador retriever. I gulped when someone rode past before shooting time and bawled him out for letting his white tee-shirt show above his camouflaged collar. I straightened my brown tie and missed nearly all of the doves.

And then, there is the plantation owner I know who goes hunting alone on horseback with a single pointer and even walks with a Brittany now and then. He said he guessed the formality was a little silly but was fun sometimes – like a masquerade.

Courtesy is important in plantation life. I recall the time I drove my weathered station wagon up to a Big House and was told not to take it to the stables and kennels. That half-mile of road was gravel, they said, and I might get my car dented up – so they took me to the stables in a Cadillac Seville.

Some of the commercial plantations are excellent imitations of private ones – some of them operating on a membership basis. In most cases they have a graduated program of hunting, ranging from freshly planted, pen-raised quail to very wild ones in almost impossible cover. The guides for such operations must frequently make quick judgements as to a client's experience and ability.

Quail management is at its best on the plantations for several reasons. First, the owners are willing to spend a great deal of money on it and will pay experts to administer it. Then, in some cases the state game managers are a big help, realizing the overflow is good for other lands and that research results can be applied elsewhere. It may be the plantations occasionally stretch the law a little in management. When I asked one owner about rattlesnakes he said there were none on his property – a bit startling since his land was in well-known snake country. He said also that there were hardly any quail predators of any kind, and his swarms of quail backed him up.

Scientific studies are likely to be done on plantations, not only because that's where the quail are easiest to find, but because plantation owners are happy to learn of the most advanced policies as they are formed. Some of the conclusions reached through plantation study may not quite fit hard-hunted public lands where coveys become itinerant because of pressure.

Those of the snagged pants and scratched gunstocks are inclined to smile a little at the affluence of Southern plantations. I keep telling myself that such hunting is too refined, but there is something special in early morning when the horses blow a little steam and the wagon creaks off on a faint trail. And there are some handlers who can sing to a dog in a way that's truly musical.

Maybe there are autoloaders in the gun rack and maybe there aren't white columns at the plantation house, but I have a feeling this whole business fits in pretty well with the Southern bobwhite scheme of things, and the birds themselves are likely to be around for a long time because of it.

CHAPTER SEVEN

The Future of Quail Hunting

by
Rocky Evans
Executive Director of Quail Unlimited

WITH THE TWENTIETH CENTURY winding down, what does the future hold for quail and quail hunters on both public and private lands? There is both good news and bad in terms of long-range management and quail-hunting opportunities.

Without question, our hunting lands are shrinking. Over a thousand acres of wetlands are drained daily, most of it being converted into big farms. This loss of critical habitat has had a dramatic effect on waterfowl populations and other wildlife species.

Unfortunately, the loss of habitat doesn't stop with the draining of wetlands. As urban sprawl continues, more and more lands will be forever lost for wildlife and outdoor uses. The small farm with brushy hedgerows and fencerows is rapidly disappearing and being replaced by incredibly intensive agricultural practices, complete with large, clean, borderless fields. Gone forever are the days that we could take a short drive, knock on a few doors, and have access to small corn and soybean fields interspersed with brushy woodlots and thinned timber. With farm foreclosures at an all-time high during the mid-80s, the agricultural crisis affecting the small and medium-scale farmer forced quail and other wildlife species to take a back seat to any financial endeavor that can help save the family farm. When you can't pay your bills, the covey-call of a bobwhite is small solace.

Enter the 1985 Farm Bill with its Conservation Reserve Program (CRP). This program has greater promise for wildlife and sportsmen than any federal program to come along in some time. CRP pays farmers and landowners to take highly erodible lands out of row-crop production and shares the cost in establishing trees, wildlife food plantings, and other cover plots. At the same time, this program will result in a number of fallow or laid-out fields which will naturally produce a variety of wild plants and cover that will provide food, cover, and shelter for quail and small game.

With the reduction of row-crops in these areas, the land will also see a relief from heavy insecticide and herbicide use that undoubtedly has played a negative role on quail and wildlife populations in the past. The Conservation Reserve Program will result in quite literally millions of acres being reestablished and maintained for at least ten years. Undoubtedly, this will provide a rebirth or rejuvenation of various wildlife species on those lands. At the same time, by increasing the carrying capacity of wildlife on those lands, the landowner will begin to see additional dollars in the forms of hunting leases and pay-by-the-day hunts. Thus, the landowner began to see in the mid-1980s that he could produce additional revenue via fur and feathers to supplement his farming operation. If there is to be a future for hunting in America, we

must continue to research ways in which wildlife can co-exist with agriculture, since the majority of lands in America are under private ownership.

There's also some good news for wildlife on the nation's public areas. In 1988, Quail Unlimited signed a Memorandum of Understanding with the Bureau of Land Management and with USDA Forest Service. For the first time in their history, the nation's largest landowners have initiated intensive quail management programs on their lands. The Forest Service alone manages over 190 million acres, all open to the public. Through its quail initiative program with Quail Unlimited, these lands will begin to see the type of habitat management that will provide vital food and cover for quail on vast acreages. Through its Memorandum of Understanding (MOU), the government must match Quail Unlimited on a dollar-for-dollar basis for all projects that QU chapters initiate on U. S. Forest Service lands and Bureau of Land Management lands. As more and more chapters are developed and established throughout the country, more funds will be available specifically for these types of projects.

The structure of Quail Unlimited allows sixty percent of its funds raised by a chapter to be spent by the chapter on projects that the chapter feels will benefit sportsmen in its local area the most. Any chapter near one of the many federally owned tracts has a wonderful opportunity to increase the carrying capacity for quail and small game and provide better opportunities for quail hunters in their areas. Obviously, this chapter network won't develop itself overnight. However, the potential to develop over 1,000 chapters by the mid-1990s is both realistic and obtainable. With Quail Unlimited chapters currently averaging just over $5,000 per chapter, this means that 1,000 chapters would create $5 million for quail in America by as early as the mid-90s. With matching federal funds via the MOU, this means up to $10 million could be available for quail management – each year.

In studying the long-term situation, we must take a look at the past rise and fall of quail numbers. On all management areas for which records have been maintained, quail populations have shown trends of gradual increase for several years followed by a severe decline before a steady up-building begins again. The severe decline in quail numbers hit during the mid to late 1970s in most parts of the country. Severe winters throughout the Midwest and northern areas reduced quail populations dramatically. Some areas rebounded quickly, while others still have not recovered. This cyclic pattern is synchronized over a great number of properties, so it cannot always be associated with an obvious change in land management. However, in comparing long term population changes from one game land to the next, we have seen that the lands with better habitat management tend to have steadier populations and *less severe drops* when a general trough occurs. There will always be bird fluctuations relating to long-term weather trends and other factors beyond the control of the land manager. The most any manager can do is to keep experimenting with habitat improvement to put his property in top shape so that it will launch a good quail population in years when the critical factors are favorable, and will carry over as many birds as possible when weather plays a negative role.

The annual cycle of quail numbers reaches the lowest point at the breeding season. From there, the population rebounds to a degree controlled by several factors acting on nest success and brood survival. Rain patterns are important, but we can only speculate as to the relationship involved. Heavy rains during the nesting season can result in washed-out nests and the drowning of new chicks, and hard rains can also cause hypothermia or other respiratory ailments of hatchlings or young chicks during this critical survival period. Down mats and sticks to chicks

when it's wet, and they catch pneumonia and die easily.

Poor quail production can also be brought on by severe drought. During this time, the inner membranes of eggs have a tendency to dry out, making it difficult if not impossible for chicks to pip their way out of the eggs. A drought period during the spring and summer will also result in low insect production that will likewise adversely affect quail populations. During the spring and summer, quail feed primarily on insects, which provide up to ninety-eight percent of their diet. Insects make up the badly needed protein and moisture for young birds. As birds are forced to travel greater distances to find this source of nutrition, they are more susceptible to exhaustion and predation. From the time quail chicks hatch until they are two to three weeks old, the birds are on the virtual cutting edge of survival daily. Periods of too much or too little rain during this time, coupled with a lack of food or cover, will produce lower populations, so it is vitally important to provide habitat for the specific *year-round needs* of quail.

TOO many land managers feel that habitat management for quail is the planting of various food plots to provide seeds during the winter months. While this is indeed important, quality habitat must also provide areas that will attract and hold insects during the spring and summer months, quality nesting cover, escape cover from predators, travel cover, and loafing cover. Quail need a *diversity* of habitat, and if that need is not met, there is little chance of any specific tract of land holding large numbers of these birds.

When speaking of a diversity in habitat, management can be complex and expensive in the form of timber thinning and creating small clearings in heavily forested areas. The planting of numerous food and cover strips throughout large tracts of land can also be expensive. Controlled burning is perhaps the most economical and useful tool for any land manager desiring to increase quail populations on his land. Prescribed burning removes the thick ground litter that often covers food that quail cannot reach by scratching. Burning also eliminates certain undesirable plants while encouraging the growth of more desirable soft plants and covers. Seeds that are split or opened by the heat will germinate better on burned-over range and will produce sprouts that will attract and hold insects in the spring and summer. Additionally, fire can actually decrease other insects that can parasitize quail. A careful, controlled burn releases the ash and minerals tied up in vegetation and stimulates the building of nitrogen in the soil. The result is a fertilizer effect for ground-layer plants.

By far, the most effective and productive prescribed burn is one that produces patchy burned areas while maintaining some cover intact. Immediately after a prescribed burn, quail are highly susceptible to various predators, especially Cooper's hawks. By totally eliminating all of the cover during this critical time, an area can lose up to an additional twenty to thirty percent of its surviving adult population to avian predators. A good object is a pattern of about seventy percent burned area, with the rest in scattered patches.

The best time of year to burn is immediately after the quail season and on cool, damp nights after a rain has stopped. By all means, select a time when the wind or high pressure fronts will disperse the smoke upward or away from road traffic. Before conducting any burn, always check with a county extension agent or a local representative from the state forestry commission. Many of these agencies provide assistance in cutting firebreaks as well as offering suggestions that will maximize the desired results.

There are many overlooked opportunities for the quail hunter to use fire beneficially. For example, some utility companies are amenable to prescribed burning in rights-of-way upon request of adjacent landowners, because prescribed burning is actually cheaper than mowing or applying herbicides in maintaining open conditions. A significant part of the future of quail hunting will lie in cooperative ventures between neighboring landowners and industrial concerns.

Libraries have been filled with information on what to plant, when to plant, where to plant, and how to plant various seeds and seedlings designed to enhance quail habitat. Without question, specifically planned food and cover strips are highly beneficial to quail and other forms of wildlife such as deer, turkey, and other small game and non-game species. Food plots such as millet, corn, sorghum, and other agricultural strips will provide both insect production in the early months and quality energy sources in the winter months.

The size and arrangement of plantings can be modified to meet individual or local needs. Quality food plots can be productive when planted in strips varying from ten to fifty feet wide and twenty to one-hundred yards long. Obviously, plots of beans, peas, corn, etc., must be larger due to raids by deer and other wildlife. Woody cover plants can be planted two to three rows wide in long strips to break up large blocks of continuous row-crops or open woods. Good places for establishing low seed plants include edges between fields and woods, well sunlit woods openings, and utility rights-of-way. Commonly recommended plot sizes for this use would range from one-eighth to one-third of an acre, with one plot per twenty or thirty acres, depending on drainage, soil type, and so forth. This way, ten small plots of less than an eighth of an acre could benefit well over 2,000 acres of land. When considering plantings for quail, remember that a large number of smaller plots with irregular edges are much more beneficial than large plots of several acres or more.

Other plants that should be incorporated into food plots would consist of legumes (members of the bean family) and other plants that provide high-energy food during the later winter months. These plants would include reseeding varieties such as: Florida beggarweed, partridge pea, and kobe or Korean lespedeza. Clovers, oats, wheat, and rye are beneficial for attracting great numbers of insects, as well as providing spring greenery for quail. Bicolor lespedeza provides an excellent winter seed and grows well on a variety of sites.

WHEN speaking of habitat management for quail, don't disregard other measures that are much less expensive and that are equally beneficial as the planting of food plots. Quail are creatures of edge – the zone between two different types of habitat. This "edge effect" can be the field edge, brush or cover edge, or forest edge. As mentioned, simple clearing of small plots in wooded areas creates valuable edge and openings for quail. This edge often means varying amounts of sunlight which produce different plants from adjoining areas. Thus, edge cover will produce several types of food, as well as hiding and nesting areas.

Let's look at simple methods that can produce more of this desirable edge. Discing of field borders will change the composition of naturally occurring plants. By discing in an irregular pattern, the land manager will create still more edge effect of his field borders. By discing at different times of the year, the manager will produce growth that will provide various age classes of food and cover. Disced strips of fifty to seventy feet, beginning in late March, will give quail better access for their broods during the summer. This shorter vegetation from the newly disced area will provide lush, green growth and will continually attract insects. Additionally, this type of simple management will further encourage natural plants that make ideal quail habitat. Ragweed, Florida beggarweed, partridge peas, Johnson grass, panic grass, and many others will flourish with this type of simple management program.

When considering inexpensive management, we should not overlook mowing. The simple mowing of certain grasses during the spring and summer is highly beneficial for quail. It keeps the ground cover open enough for brood habitat, yet stimulates enough to grow and attract insects. Mowing is also helpful in keeping down undesirable brush around some fields. In wooded habitat, the bush-hogging of thick hardwood sprouts can be beneficial. In fact, burning of mowed brush can

encourage some of the better wild legumes, such as milk pea, to spread more abundantly.

Simply by lightly disturbing the soil and slightly altering existing habitat, we can create valuable habitat for quail on a minimum budget. Through light fertilization of these slightly altered habitats, we can stimulate the growth of natural plants that will attract and hold the number of quail we're looking for.

Habitat needs for quail, however, vary greatly, depending on the geographical area. For instance, in the Southwest, we should be more concerned with establishing man-made brushpiles and watering holes known as "guzzlers." Time and money is best spent on servicing guzzlers and fencing off areas to prevent cattle from tromping vital habitat along stream edges. In the Midwest, many quail hunters (and QU members) are involved in purchasing equipment to help re-establish native grasslands. Additionally, root plows are used extensively to keep farmers from pushing up hedgerows or cutting trees that provide protection from harsh winters. In the Southeast, the accent is on establishing numerous food and cover strips along with seasonal discing and controlled burning. Again, the idea is to determine the specific habitat needs of your area and address your management program to meet those concerns.

Remember that a quail weighs about six ounces, and he'd rather walk than fly. Large, borderless fields present an impenetrable barrier to quail and will prevent them from using such areas. In a nutshell, without food, constant shelter, and water, there is little chance of finding huntable populations of quail in *any* area. Quail have an uncanny ability to bounce back after harsh weather. If the habitat is in place to assist that recovery, then you will be better able to attract and hold sizable populations of this winged wonder.

S INCE the turn of the century, quail have been one of the most popular game bird species found in America. However, with land use changes we have seen over the last ten to twenty years, more and more hunters are faced with the problem of finding a suitable place to hunt. As a result, we have seen a tremendous increase in the number of preserves and pay-by-the-day hunts.

Any chapter on the bobwhite's future has to recognize that these places exist and, without question, the hunting preserve will provide marvelous opportunities for those who can afford to pay for a hunt on a daily, weekly, or corporate basis. For the most part, shooting preserves can provide high quality, fast-action gunning for any bird hunter. The preserve seasons generally run from early October until the last of March, depending on the state. Preserves are an excellent way to start a youngster in quail hunting; they offer good dog work and lots of shooting that will more likely make a favorable impression on a youngster his first time out. We all remember and even appreciate those days of endless trudging through clearcuts, woodlots, and even productive-looking cover without a point the entire day. That's part of hunting. But with a less-developed sense of appreciation for the outdoors, a more desirable impression and memory of the first hunt will be made if the youngster is finally able to score a hit or two. Preserves also offer an excellent opportunity to get young dogs into birds under hunting situations.

But let's face it, preserves aren't for everyone. Not everyone can afford the daily rates they must charge to ensure a successful financial operation, and many still long for the cardiac rush produced by the unexpected wild coveys. But quality preserves certainly have their place and no doubt will play a key role in the quail hunting many will see in the future.

As the number of preserves across the country increases, along with the habitat loss each year, some are speculating that quail hunting will become simply a rich man's sport. On the surface that certainly looks to be the case. However, those hunters who are willing to work a little harder for their sport, drive a little longer, and knock on a few more doors will continue to see their efforts rewarded. As I mentioned, in addition to the wildlife management areas run by each state's fish and game agency, literally millions of acres are now being developed for quail hunters by the Bureau of Land Management, U.S. Forest Service, and Quail Unlimited. This situation didn't deteriorate overnight, and it is highly unlikely that things will turn around overnight, either. However, many fish and game agencies are now hearing from organized bird hunters and have redirected funding to include specific quail management plans on their wildlife management areas.

Additionally, landowners are beginning to see more value in wildlife on the lands as a result of a rebirth of enthusiasm in quail hunting. Perhaps the most important role to be played by Quail Unlimited will be in the area of education, information, and public awareness. By teaching landowners to

manage with wildlife in mind, then making certain assistance programs available such as free seed, farm equipment, and volunteer labor, we see that more and more landowners are beginning to manage with the specific needs of quail and wildlife in mind. Ducks Unlimited began with the same-type need in the early 1930s but really began to blossom during the 1970s. With this same interest and chapter program in Quail Unlimited, funds will be more readily available to maximize the carrying capacity of lands available for wildlife use.

Quail Unlimited was founded in October of 1981 and since that time has become a leader in quail and upland game bird management and awareness. If I can blow our own horn a little, I'd like to say that from its earliest inception, QU's leaders saw the need to manage habitat on the local, state, and national levels and in as many areas as possible. Since that time, the organization has initiated youth projects designed to educate and interest youngsters in the true needs of wildlife. Its youth program, Project Y.I.E.L.D. (Youth Involvement and Educational Land Development) has helped educate thousands of youngsters while encouraging them to plant small plots for wildlife. And we think this is vital to the future of quail hunting: a generation of educated quail hunters.

We must constantly strive to learn new ways to productively and economically manage for this marvelous game bird. At the same time, we must study and better learn of the relationships between agricultural practices and chemicals and even other wildlife species. Through its chapter program, the organization is able to disseminate this information to the farmer, land manager, hunting club, and sportsman. By offering assistance programs such as free seed and farm implements, the organization is able to assist local groups and clubs as well as landowners with projects on the local level. Through its programs, all designed to meet various habitat and management programs on the local level, we feel

QU will be able to address the individual needs of quail from coast to coast.

No, the situation is far from dismal. In fact, through increased awareness sportsmen, landowners, and state and federal agencies are now addressing the specific needs of quail across the United States. With care and attention to his specific needs, this six-ounce wonder will continue to provide us with thrills that only a bird hunter can appreciate and will continue to be known as the "Prince of Game Birds."

•   •   •

I have borrowed liberally from a fine work on quail management, and it occurs to me you may want to know more than I've told you. If so, please consult this book:

Landers, J. Larry, and Mueller, Brad S., 1986. *Bobwhite Quail Management: A Habitat Approach*. In cooperation between Tall Timbers Research Station and Quail Unlimited.